THE AMATEURS

EDITOR AND ASSOCIATE PUBLISHER: ERIC REYNOLDS
DESIGN: EMORY LIU
PRODUCTION: PAUL BARESH
PUBLISHER: GARY GROTH

FANTAGRAPHICS BOOKS, INC.
SEATTLE, WASHINGTON, USA

ISBN 978-1-60699-734-5

FIRST PRINTING: JUNE, 2014
PRINTED IN HONG KONG

FANTAGRAPHICS BOOKS WOULD LIKE TO THANK: RANDALL BETHUNE · BIG PLANET
COMICS · BLACK HOOK PRESS, JAPAN · NICK CAPETILLO · KEVIN CZAPIEWSKI · JOHN
DIBELLO · JUAN MANUEL DOMÍNGUEZ · MATHIEU DOUBLET · DAN EVANS III · THOMAS
EYKEMANS · SCOTT FRITSCH-HAMMES · COCO AND EDDIE GORODETSKY · KAREN GREEN
· TED HAYCRAFT · EDUARDO TAKEO "LIZARKEO" IGARASHI · NEVDON JAMGOCHIAN
· ANDY KOOPMANS · PHILIP NEL · VANESSA PALACIOS · KURT SAYENGA · ANNE LISE
ROSTGAARD SCHMIDT · CHRISTIAN SCHREMSER · SECRET HEADQUARTERS · PAUL VAN
DIJKEN · MUNGO VAN KRIMPEN-HALL · JASON AARON WONG · THOMAS ZIMMERMANN

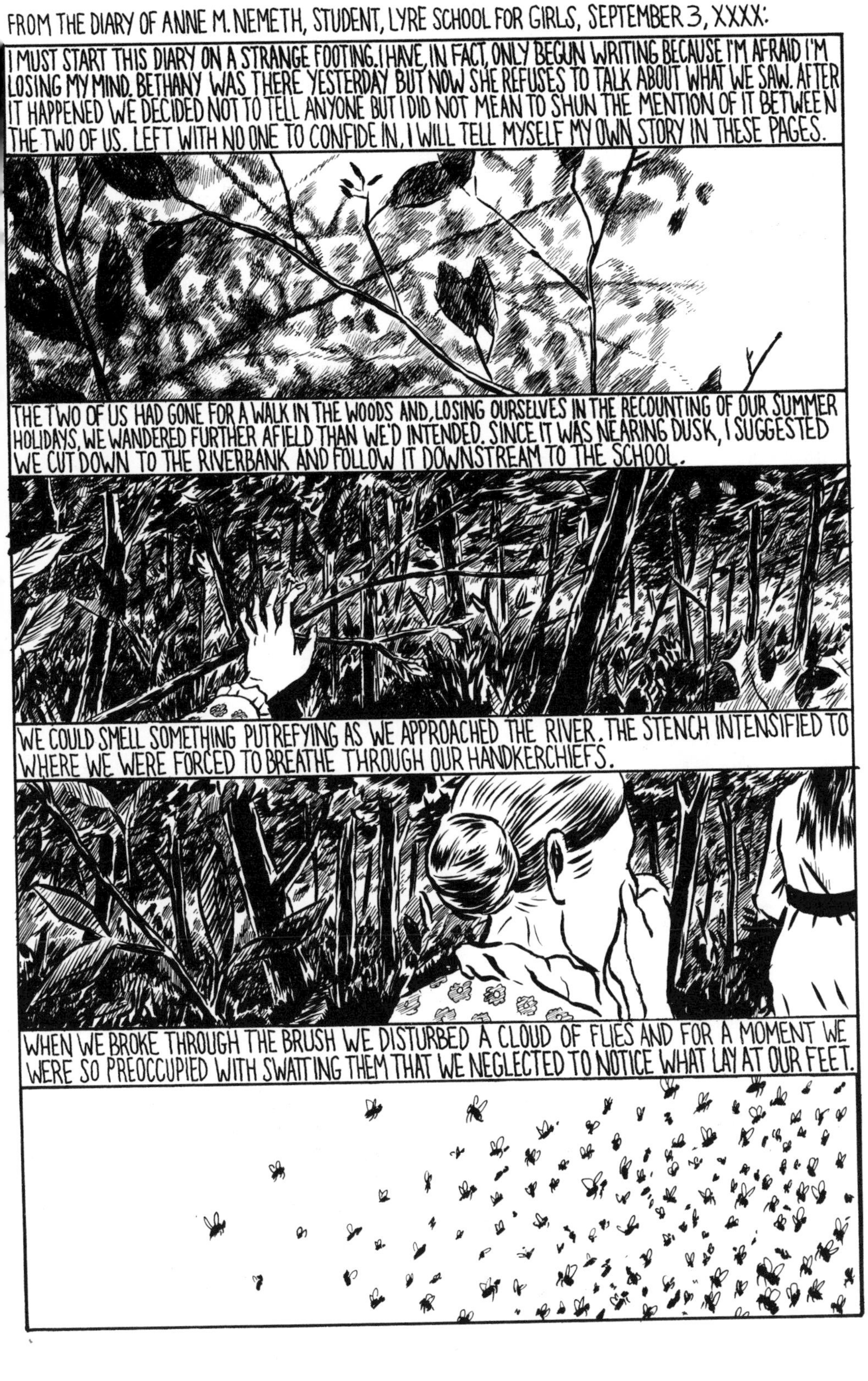
FROM THE DIARY OF ANNE M. NEMETH, STUDENT, LYRE SCHOOL FOR GIRLS, SEPTEMBER 3, XXXX:
I MUST START THIS DIARY ON A STRANGE FOOTING. I HAVE, IN FACT, ONLY BEGUN WRITING BECAUSE I'M AFRAID I'M LOSING MY MIND. BETHANY WAS THERE YESTERDAY BUT NOW SHE REFUSES TO TALK ABOUT WHAT WE SAW. AFTER IT HAPPENED WE DECIDED NOT TO TELL ANYONE BUT I DID NOT MEAN TO SHUN THE MENTION OF IT BETWEEN THE TWO OF US. LEFT WITH NO ONE TO CONFIDE IN, I WILL TELL MYSELF MY OWN STORY IN THESE PAGES.
THE TWO OF US HAD GONE FOR A WALK IN THE WOODS AND, LOSING OURSELVES IN THE RECOUNTING OF OUR SUMMER HOLIDAYS, WE WANDERED FURTHER AFIELD THAN WE'D INTENDED. SINCE IT WAS NEARING DUSK, I SUGGESTED WE CUT DOWN TO THE RIVERBANK AND FOLLOW IT DOWNSTREAM TO THE SCHOOL.
WE COULD SMELL SOMETHING PUTREFYING AS WE APPROACHED THE RIVER. THE STENCH INTENSIFIED TO WHERE WE WERE FORCED TO BREATHE THROUGH OUR HANDKERCHIEFS.
WHEN WE BROKE THROUGH THE BRUSH WE DISTURBED A CLOUD OF FLIES AND FOR A MOMENT WE WERE SO PREOCCUPIED WITH SWATTING THEM THAT WE NEGLECTED TO NOTICE WHAT LAY AT OUR FEET.

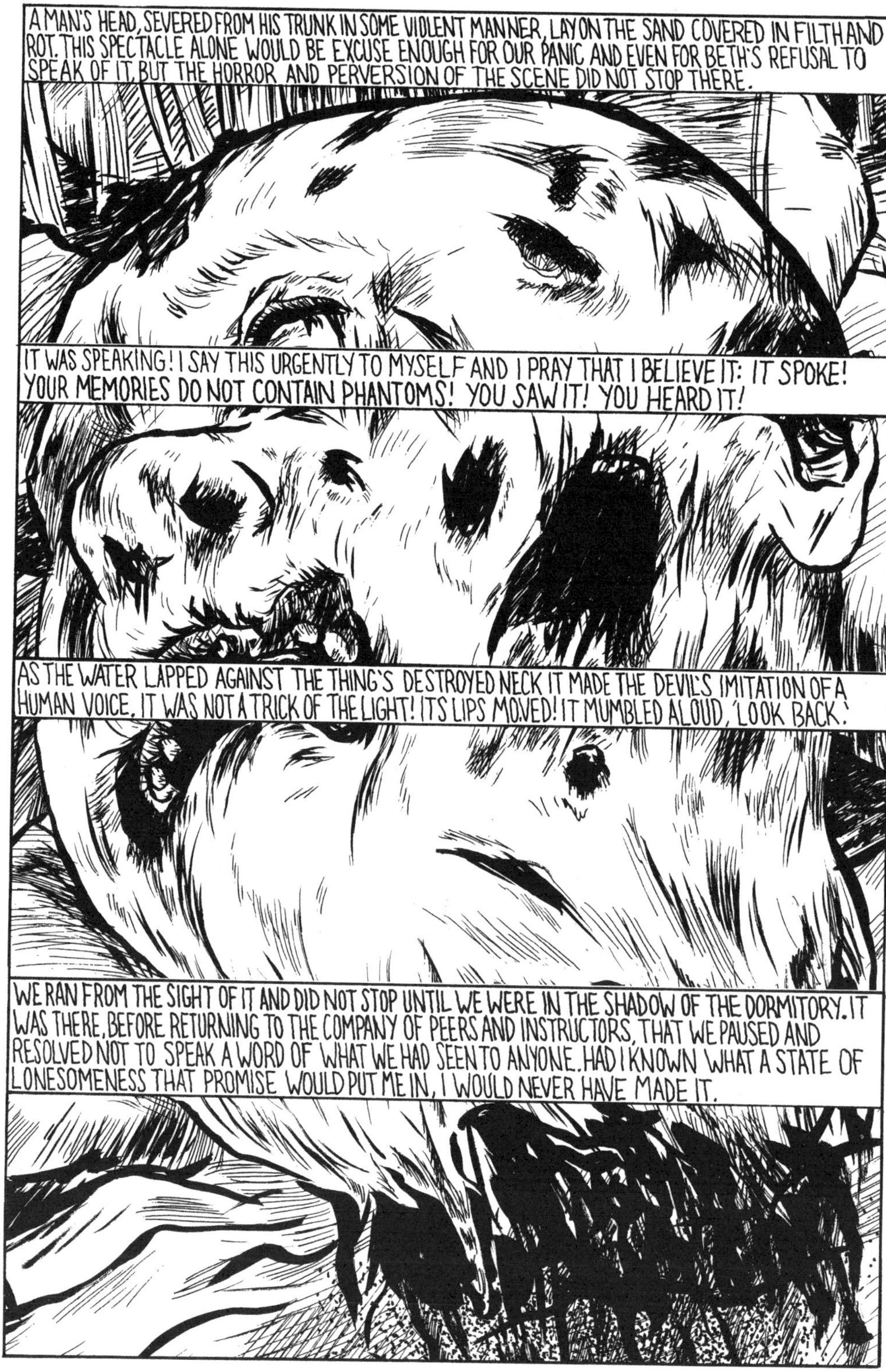
A MAN'S HEAD, SEVERED FROM HIS TRUNK IN SOME VIOLENT MANNER, LAY ON THE SAND COVERED IN FILTH AND ROT. THIS SPECTACLE ALONE WOULD BE EXCUSE ENOUGH FOR OUR PANIC AND EVEN FOR BETH'S REFUSAL TO SPEAK OF IT, BUT THE HORROR AND PERVERSION OF THE SCENE DID NOT STOP THERE.
IT WAS SPEAKING! I SAY THIS URGENTLY TO MYSELF AND I PRAY THAT I BELIEVE IT: IT SPOKE! YOUR MEMORIES DO NOT CONTAIN PHANTOMS! YOU SAW IT! YOU HEARD IT!
AS THE WATER LAPPED AGAINST THE THING'S DESTROYED NECK IT MADE THE DEVIL'S IMITATION OF A HUMAN VOICE. IT WAS NOT A TRICK OF THE LIGHT! ITS LIPS MOVED! IT MUMBLED ALOUD, 'LOOK BACK.'
WE RAN FROM THE SIGHT OF IT AND DID NOT STOP UNTIL WE WERE IN THE SHADOW OF THE DORMITORY. IT WAS THERE, BEFORE RETURNING TO THE COMPANY OF PEERS AND INSTRUCTORS, THAT WE PAUSED AND RESOLVED NOT TO SPEAK A WORD OF WHAT WE HAD SEEN TO ANYONE. HAD I KNOWN WHAT A STATE OF LONESOMENESS THAT PROMISE WOULD PUT ME IN, I WOULD NEVER HAVE MADE IT.

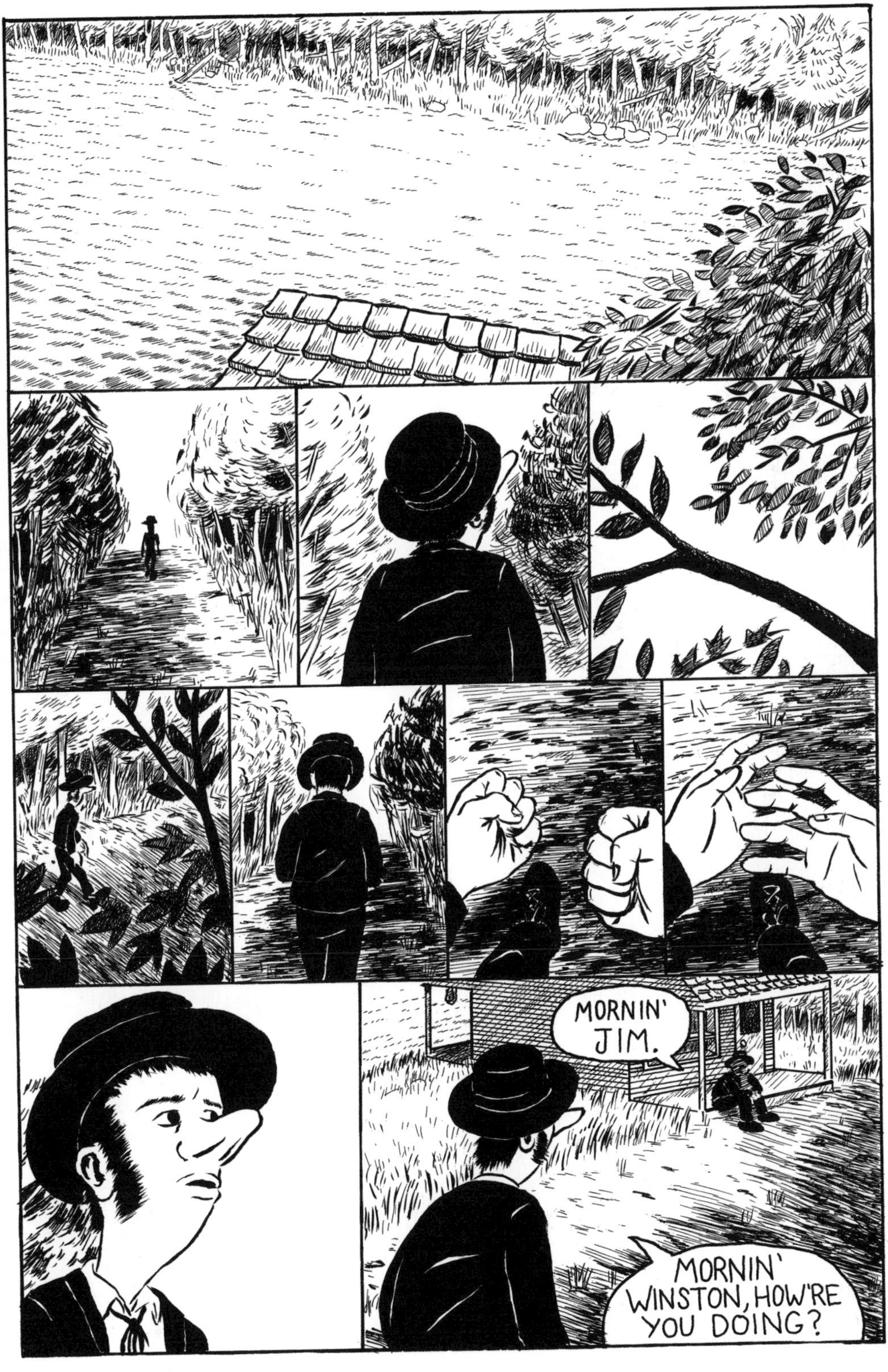
MORNIN' JIM.
MORNIN' WINSTON, HOW'RE YOU DOING?

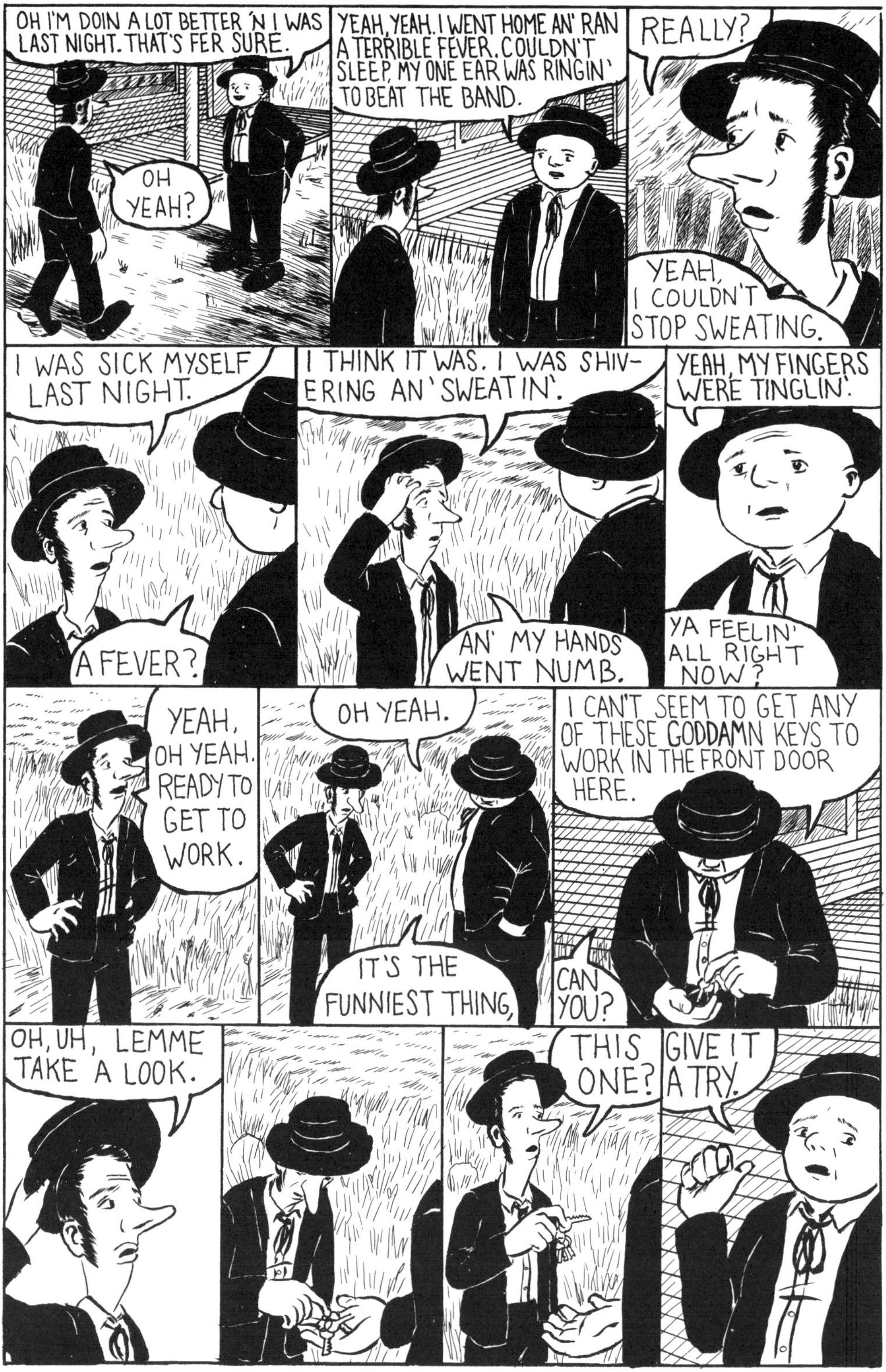

OH I'M DOIN A LOT BETTER 'N I WAS LAST NIGHT. THAT'S FER SURE.
OH YEAH?
YEAH, YEAH. I WENT HOME AN' RAN A TERRIBLE FEVER. COULDN'T SLEEP, MY ONE EAR WAS RINGIN' TO BEAT THE BAND.
REALLY?
YEAH, I COULDN'T STOP SWEATING.
I WAS SICK MYSELF LAST NIGHT.
A FEVER?
I THINK IT WAS. I WAS SHIVERING AN' SWEATIN'.
AN' MY HANDS WENT NUMB.
YEAH, MY FINGERS WERE TINGLIN'.
YA FEELIN' ALL RIGHT NOW?
YEAH, OH YEAH. READY TO GET TO WORK.
OH YEAH.
IT'S THE FUNNIEST THING,
I CAN'T SEEM TO GET ANY OF THESE GODDAMN KEYS TO WORK IN THE FRONT DOOR HERE.
CAN YOU?
OH, UH, LEMME TAKE A LOOK.
THIS ONE?
GIVE IT A TRY.

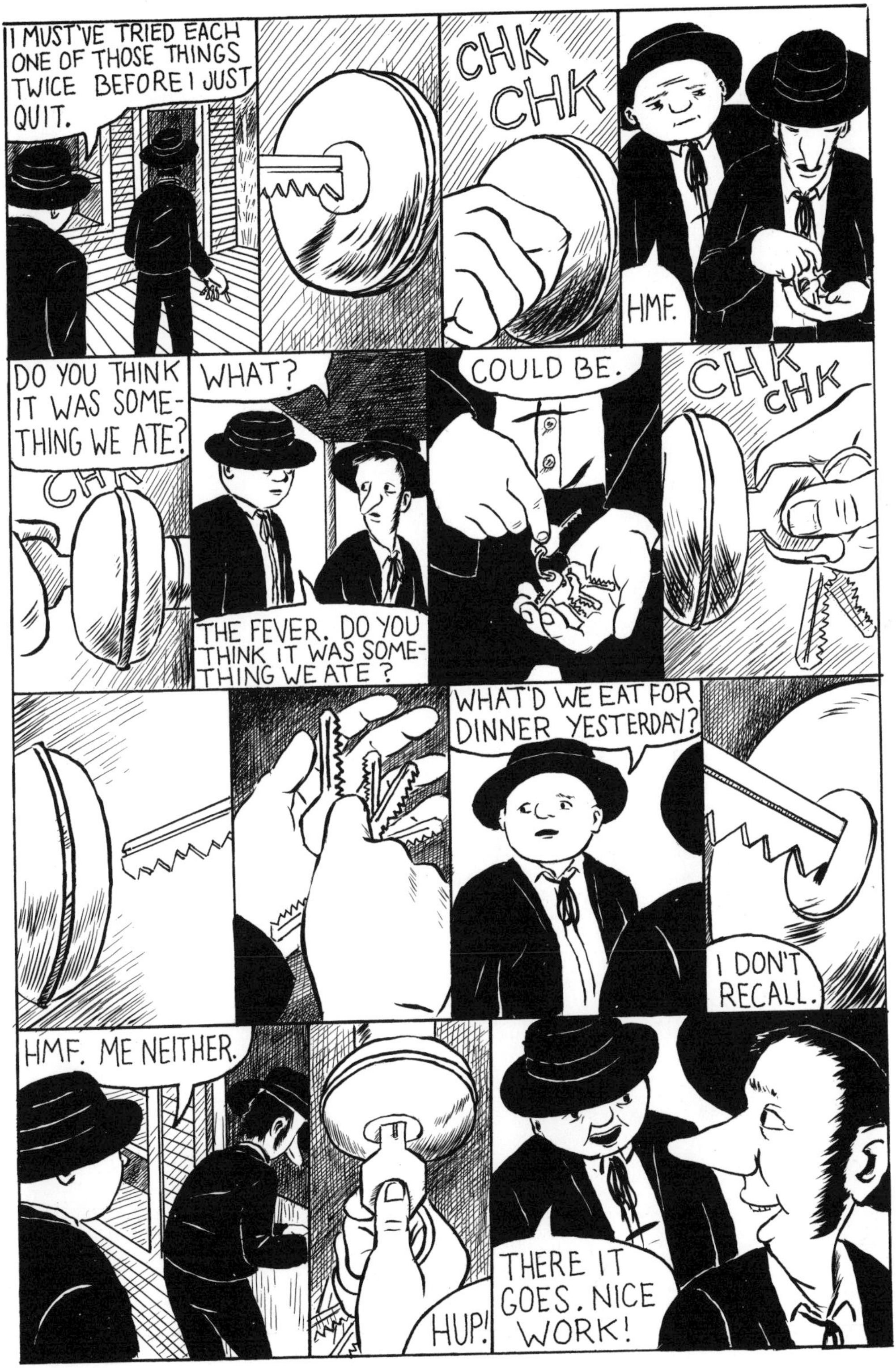
I MUST'VE TRIED EACH ONE OF THOSE THINGS TWICE BEFORE I JUST QUIT.
CHK CHK
HMF.
DO YOU THINK IT WAS SOMETHING WE ATE?
WHAT?
THE FEVER. DO YOU THINK IT WAS SOMETHING WE ATE?
COULD BE.
CHK CHK
WHAT'D WE EAT FOR DINNER YESTERDAY?
I DON'T RECALL.
HMF. ME NEITHER.
HUP!
THERE IT GOES. NICE WORK!

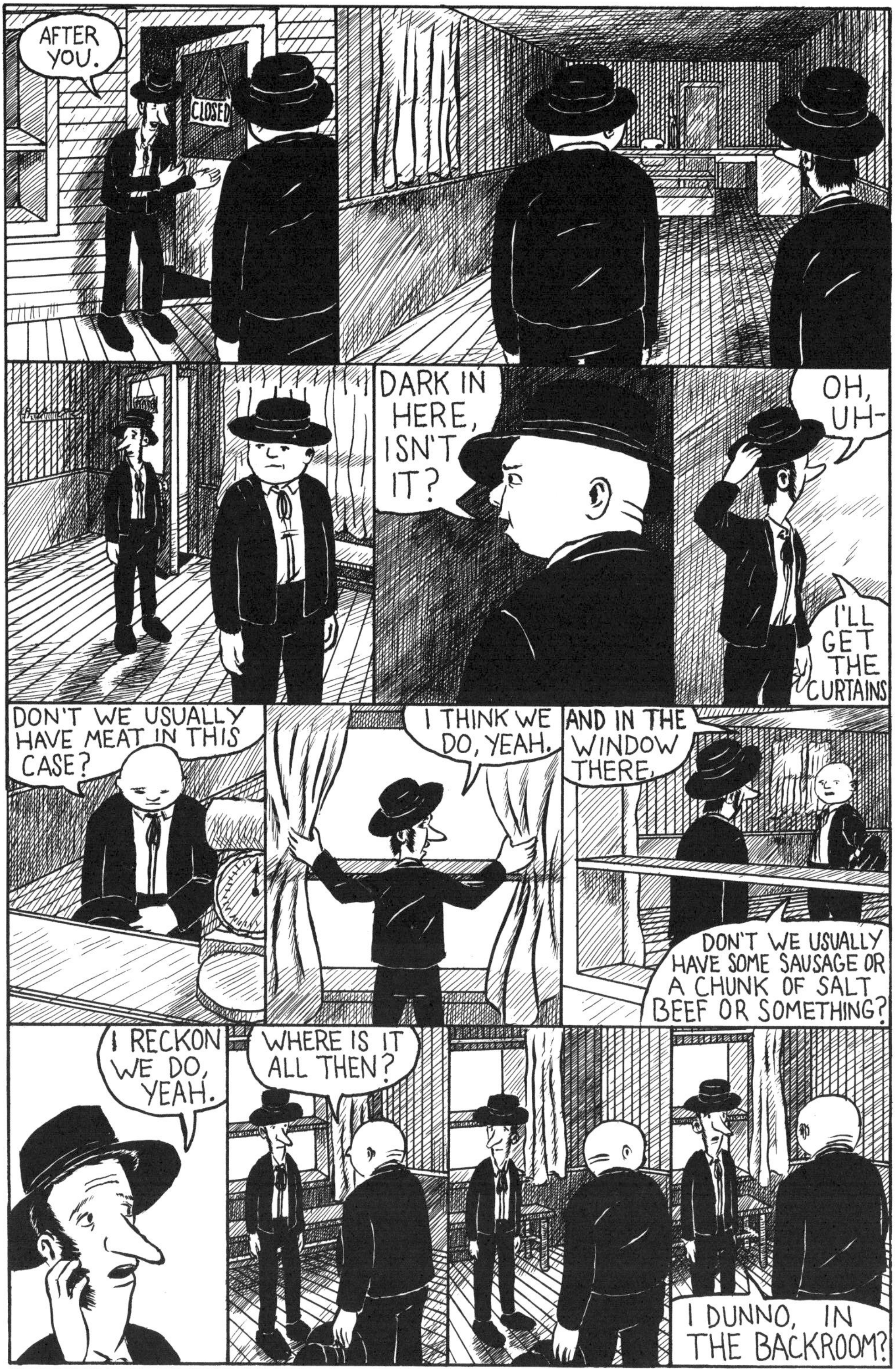
AFTER YOU.
CLOSED
DARK IN HERE, ISN'T IT?
OH, UH-
I'LL GET THE CURTAINS
DON'T WE USUALLY HAVE MEAT IN THIS CASE?
I THINK WE DO, YEAH.
AND IN THE WINDOW THERE,
DON'T WE USUALLY HAVE SOME SAUSAGE OR A CHUNK OF SALT BEEF OR SOMETHING?
I RECKON WE DO, YEAH.
WHERE IS IT ALL THEN?
I DUNNO, IN THE BACKROOM?

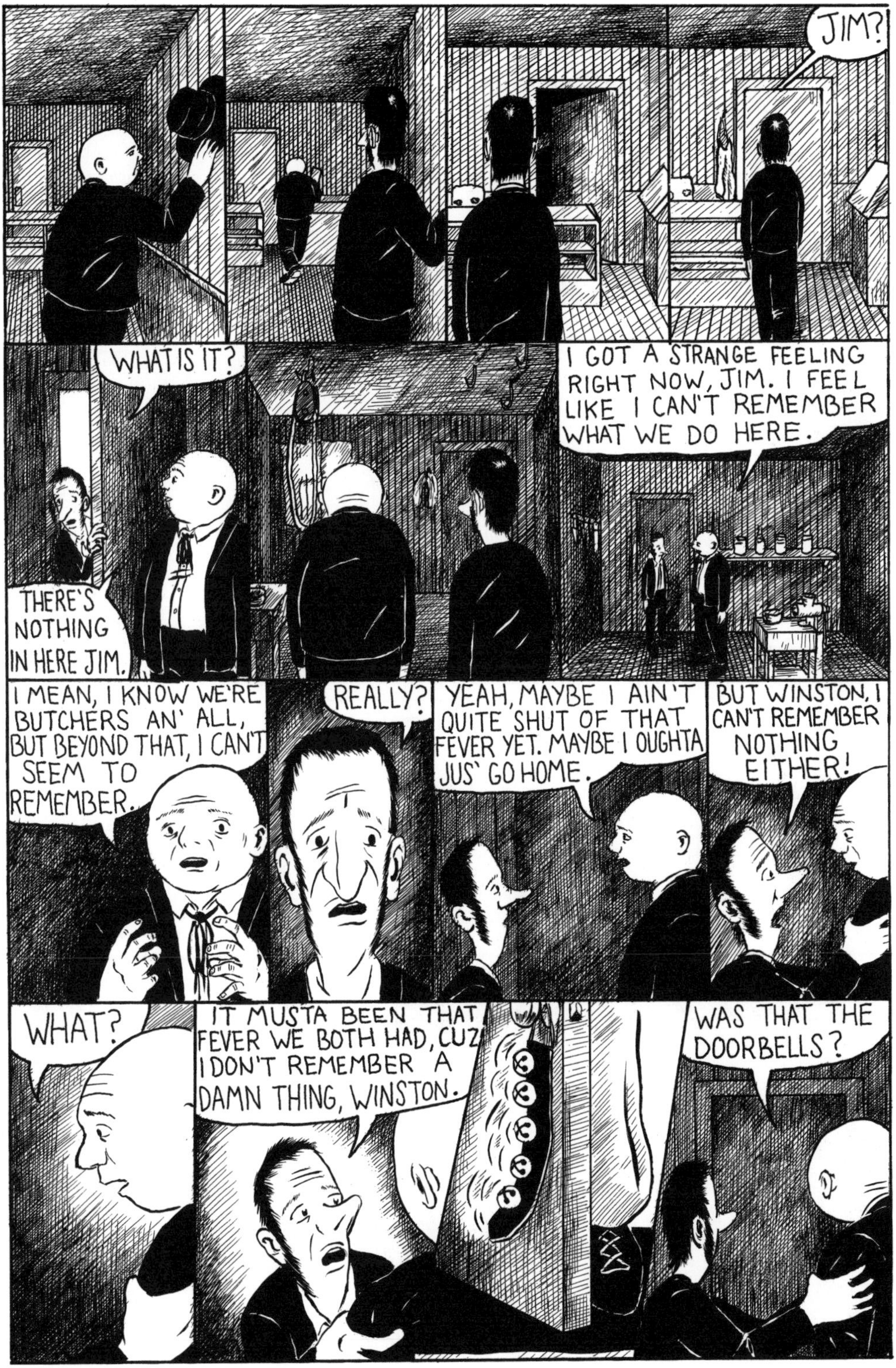
JIM?
WHAT IS IT?
THERE'S NOTHING IN HERE JIM.
I GOT A STRANGE FEELING RIGHT NOW, JIM. I FEEL LIKE I CAN'T REMEMBER WHAT WE DO HERE.
I MEAN, I KNOW WE'RE BUTCHERS AN' ALL, BUT BEYOND THAT, I CAN'T SEEM TO REMEMBER.
REALLY?
YEAH, MAYBE I AIN'T QUITE SHUT OF THAT FEVER YET. MAYBE I OUGHTA JUS' GO HOME.
BUT WINSTON, I CAN'T REMEMBER NOTHING EITHER!
WHAT?
IT MUSTA BEEN THAT FEVER WE BOTH HAD, CUZ I DON'T REMEMBER A DAMN THING, WINSTON.
WAS THAT THE DOORBELLS?

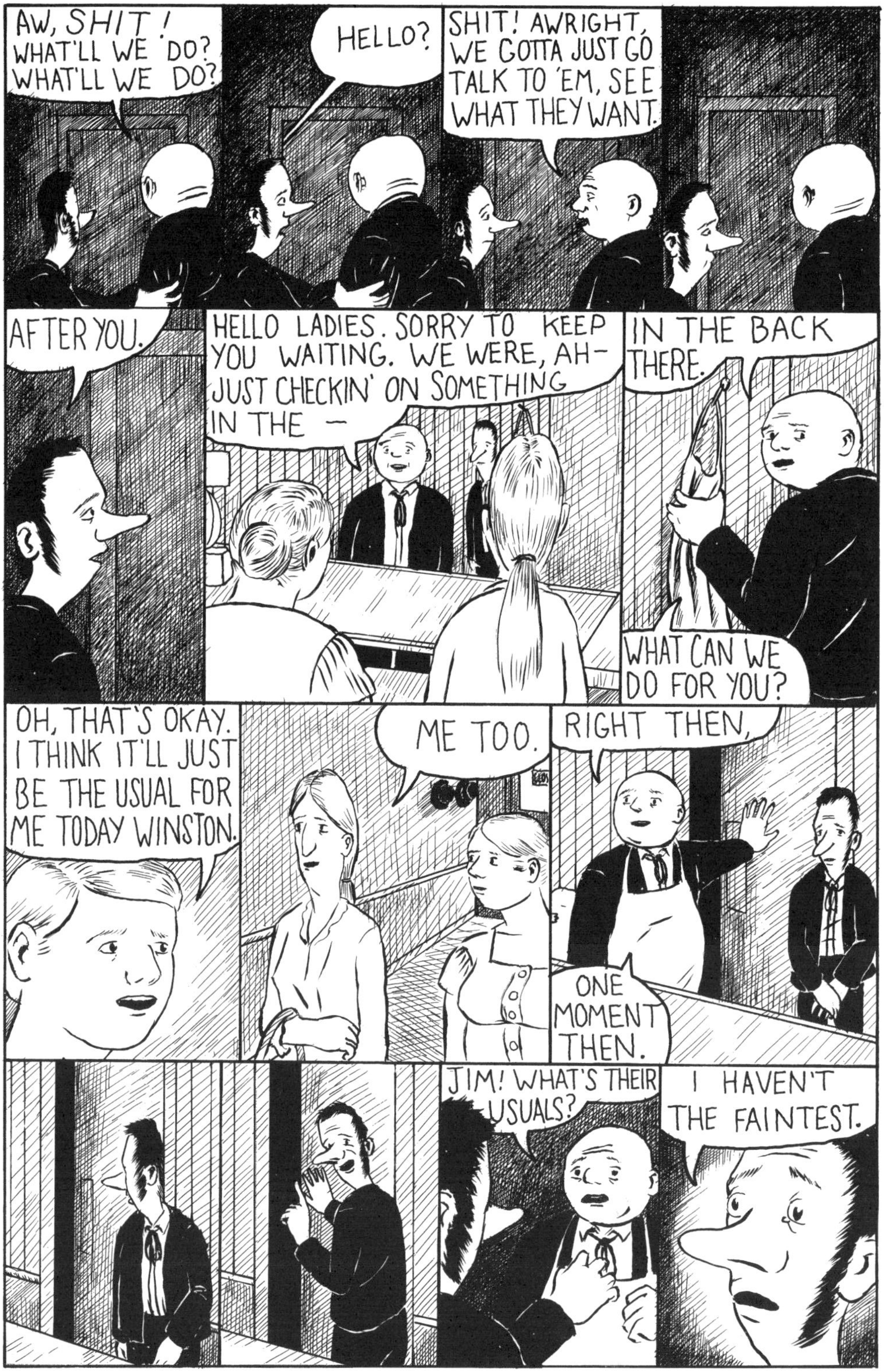
AW, SHIT! WHAT'LL WE DO? WHAT'LL WE DO?
HELLO?
SHIT! AWRIGHT, WE GOTTA JUST GO TALK TO 'EM, SEE WHAT THEY WANT.
AFTER YOU.
HELLO LADIES. SORRY TO KEEP YOU WAITING. WE WERE, AH- JUST CHECKIN' ON SOMETHING IN THE —
IN THE BACK THERE.
WHAT CAN WE DO FOR YOU?
OH, THAT'S OKAY. I THINK IT'LL JUST BE THE USUAL FOR ME TODAY WINSTON.
ME TOO.
RIGHT THEN,
ONE MOMENT THEN.
JIM! WHAT'S THEIR USUALS?
I HAVEN'T THE FAINTEST.

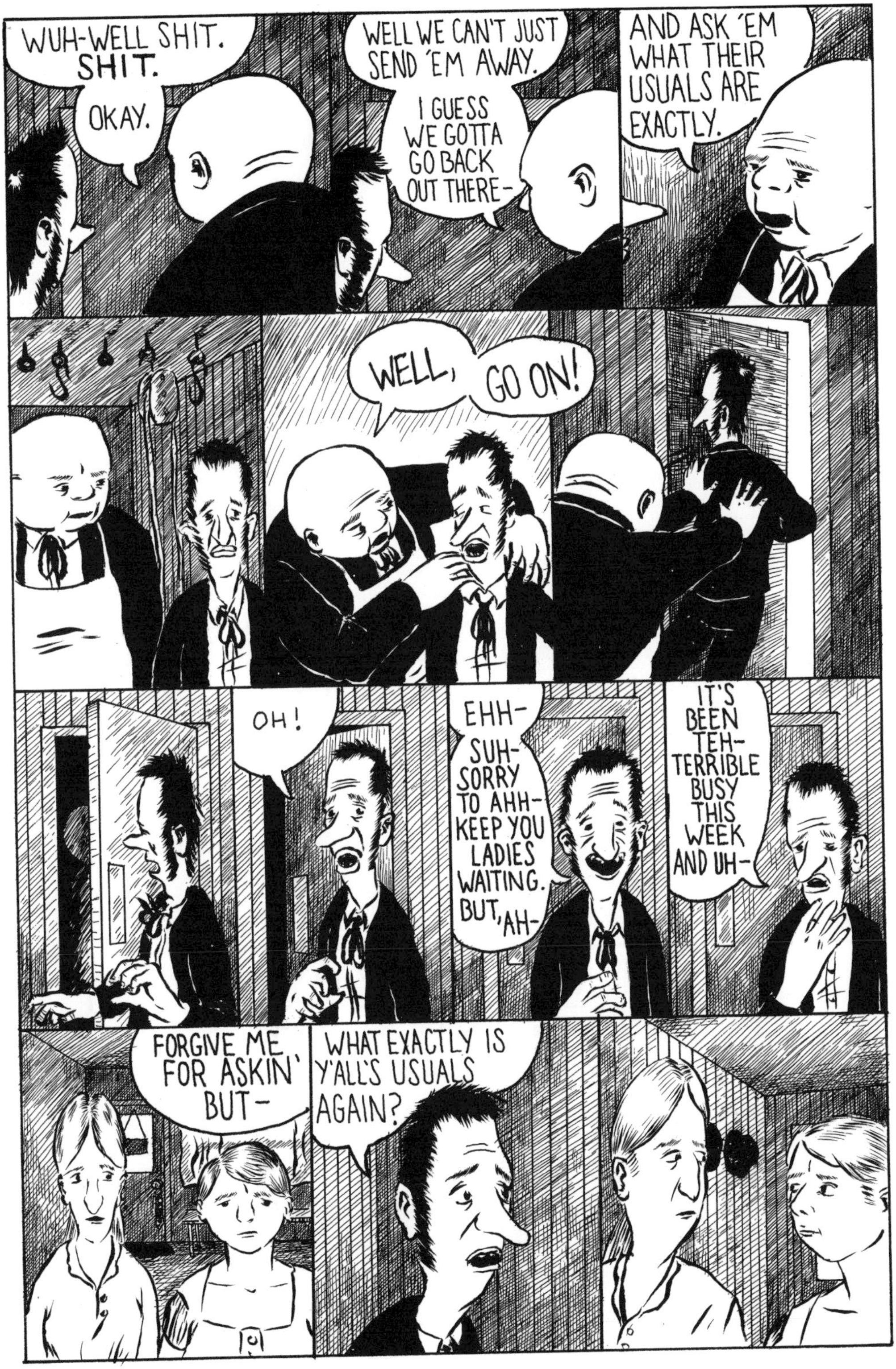
WUH-WELL SHIT.
SHIT.
OKAY.
WELL WE CAN'T JUST SEND 'EM AWAY.
I GUESS WE GOTTA GO BACK OUT THERE-
AND ASK 'EM WHAT THEIR USUALS ARE EXACTLY.
WELL,
GO ON!
OH!
EHH-
SUH-SORRY TO AHH-KEEP YOU LADIES WAITING.
BUT, AH-
IT'S BEEN TEH-TERRIBLE BUSY THIS WEEK AND UH-
FORGIVE ME FOR ASKIN' BUT-
WHAT EXACTLY IS Y'ALL'S USUALS AGAIN?

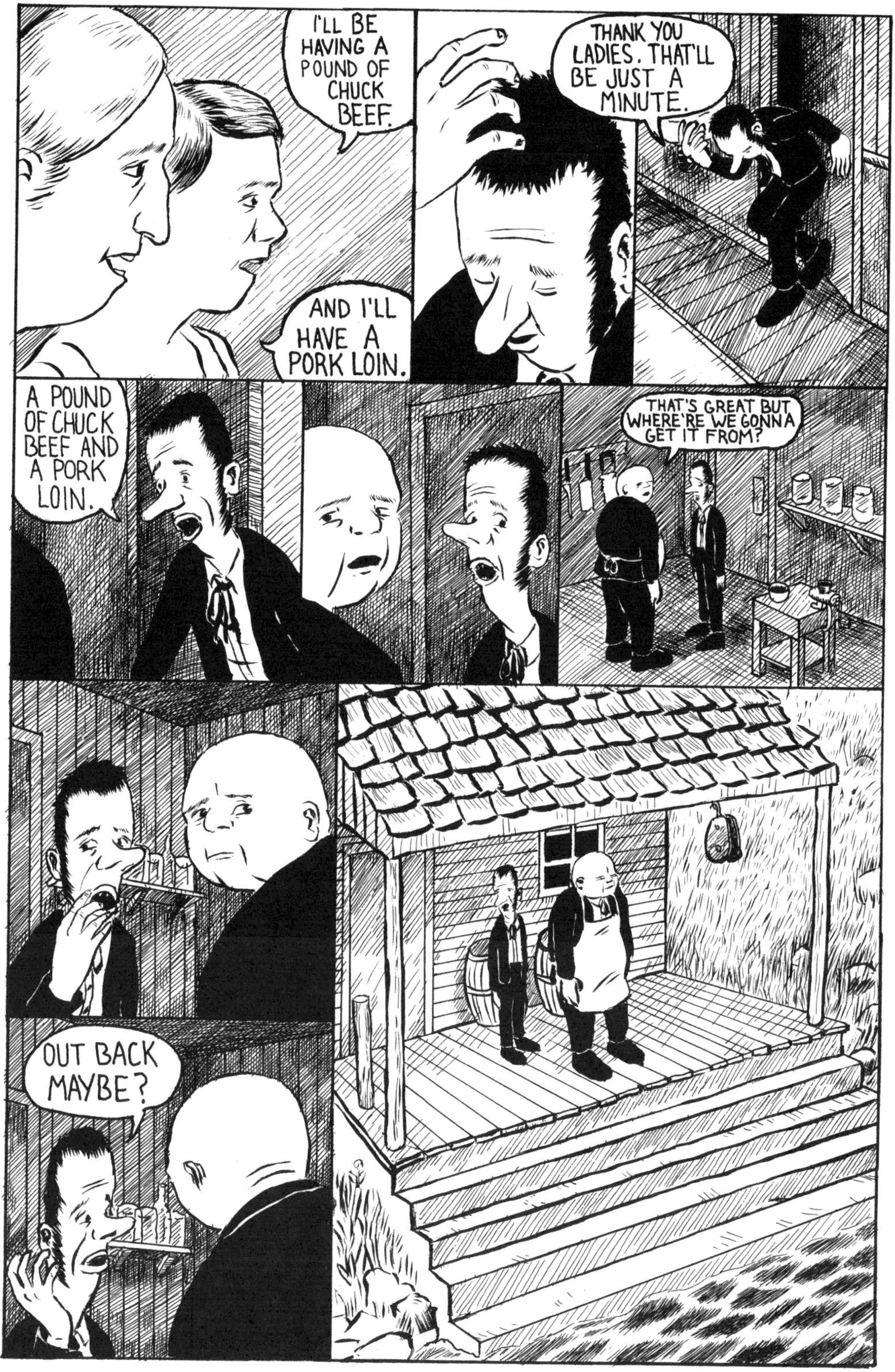
I'LL BE HAVING A POUND OF CHUCK BEEF.
AND I'LL HAVE A PORK LOIN.
THANK YOU LADIES. THAT'LL BE JUST A MINUTE.
A POUND OF CHUCK BEEF AND A PORK LOIN.
THAT'S GREAT BUT WHERE'RE WE GONNA GET IT FROM?
OUT BACK MAYBE?

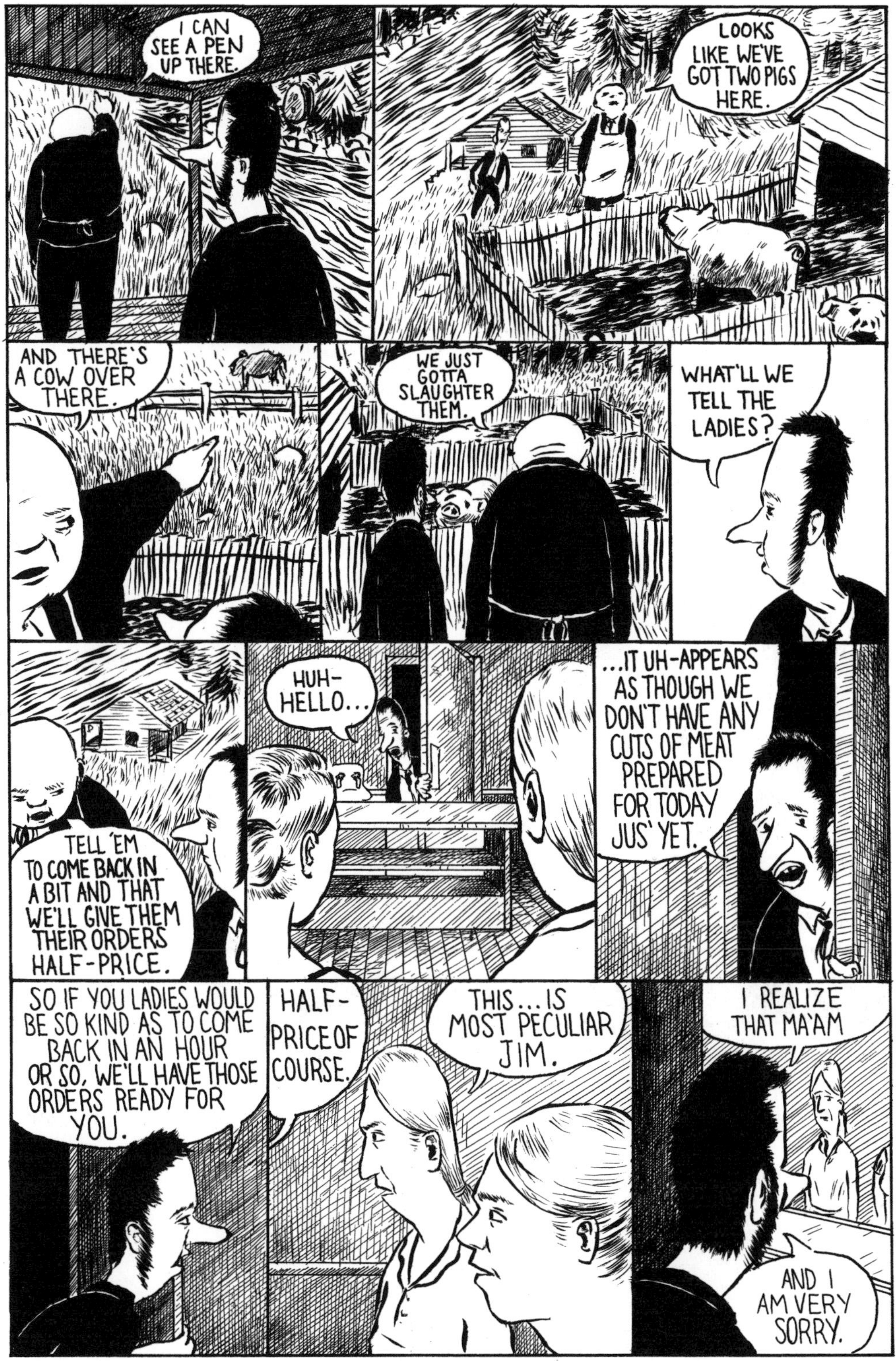
I CAN SEE A PEN UP THERE.
LOOKS LIKE WE'VE GOT TWO PIGS HERE.
AND THERE'S A COW OVER THERE.
WE JUST GOTTA SLAUGHTER THEM.
WHAT'LL WE TELL THE LADIES?
TELL 'EM TO COME BACK IN A BIT AND THAT WE'LL GIVE THEM THEIR ORDERS HALF-PRICE.
HUH-HELLO...
...IT UH-APPEARS AS THOUGH WE DON'T HAVE ANY CUTS OF MEAT PREPARED FOR TODAY JUS' YET.
SO IF YOU LADIES WOULD BE SO KIND AS TO COME BACK IN AN HOUR OR SO, WE'LL HAVE THOSE ORDERS READY FOR YOU.
HALF-PRICE OF COURSE.
THIS... IS MOST PECULIAR JIM.
I REALIZE THAT MA'AM
AND I AM VERY SORRY.

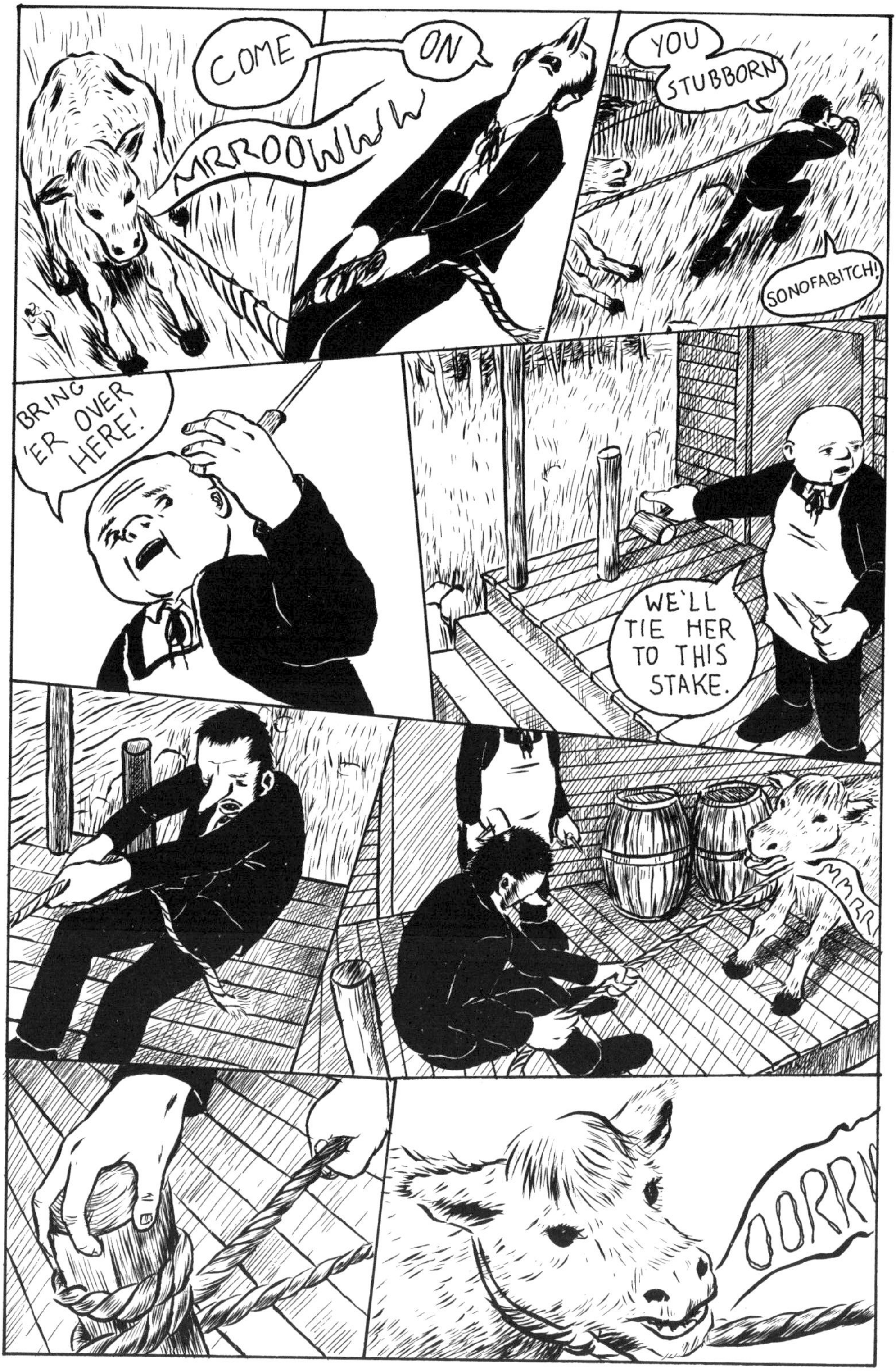
COME
ON
MRROOWWW
YOU
STUBBORN
SONOFABITCH!
BRING 'ER OVER HERE!
WE'LL TIE HER TO THIS STAKE.
MMRR
OORR

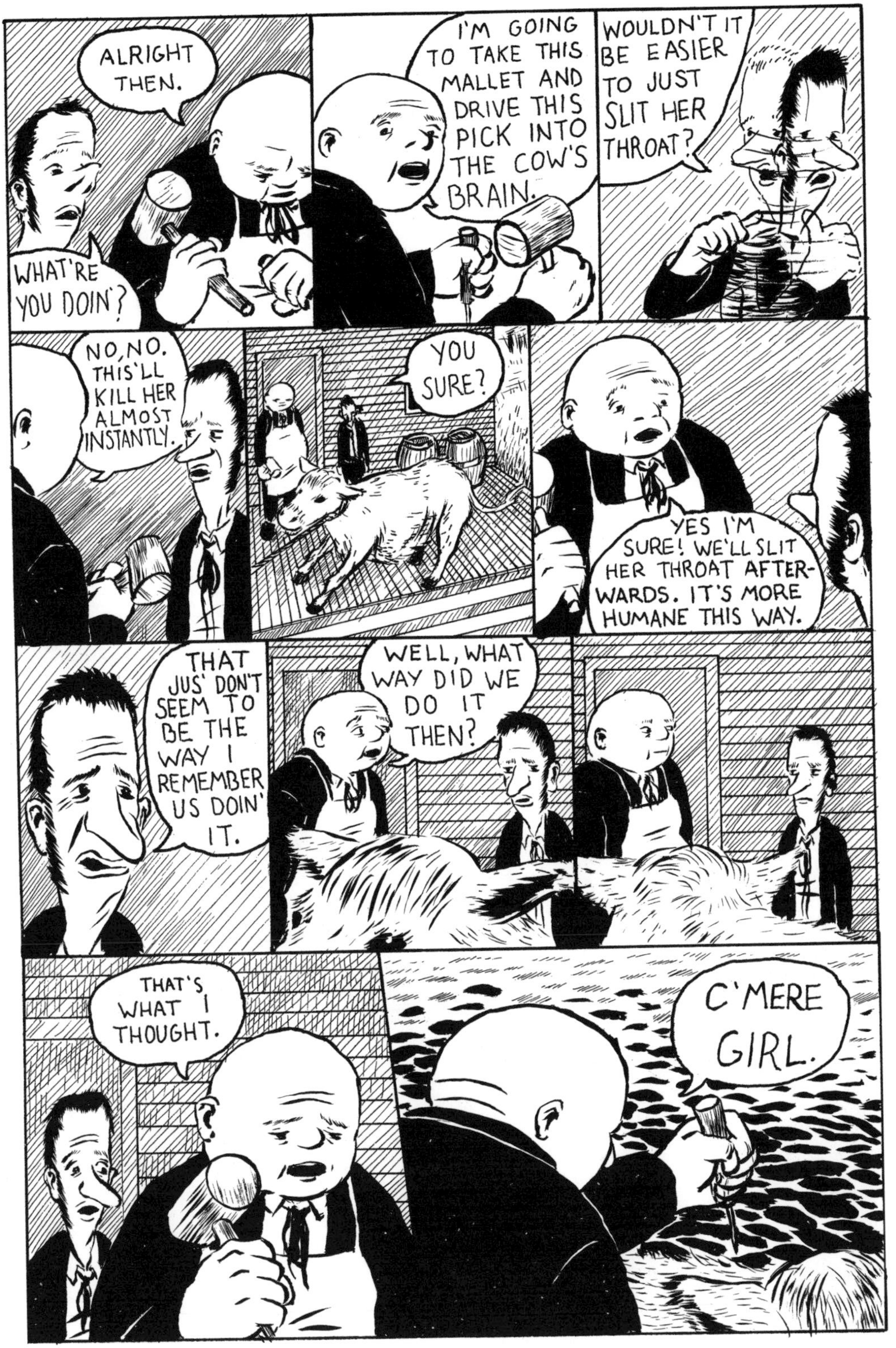
ALRIGHT THEN.
WHAT'RE YOU DOIN'?
I'M GOING TO TAKE THIS MALLET AND DRIVE THIS PICK INTO THE COW'S BRAIN.
WOULDN'T IT BE EASIER TO JUST SLIT HER THROAT?
NO, NO. THIS'LL KILL HER ALMOST INSTANTLY.
YOU SURE?
YES I'M SURE! WE'LL SLIT HER THROAT AFTER-WARDS. IT'S MORE HUMANE THIS WAY.
THAT JUS' DON'T SEEM TO BE THE WAY I REMEMBER US DOIN' IT.
WELL, WHAT WAY DID WE DO IT THEN?
THAT'S WHAT I THOUGHT.
C'MERE GIRL.

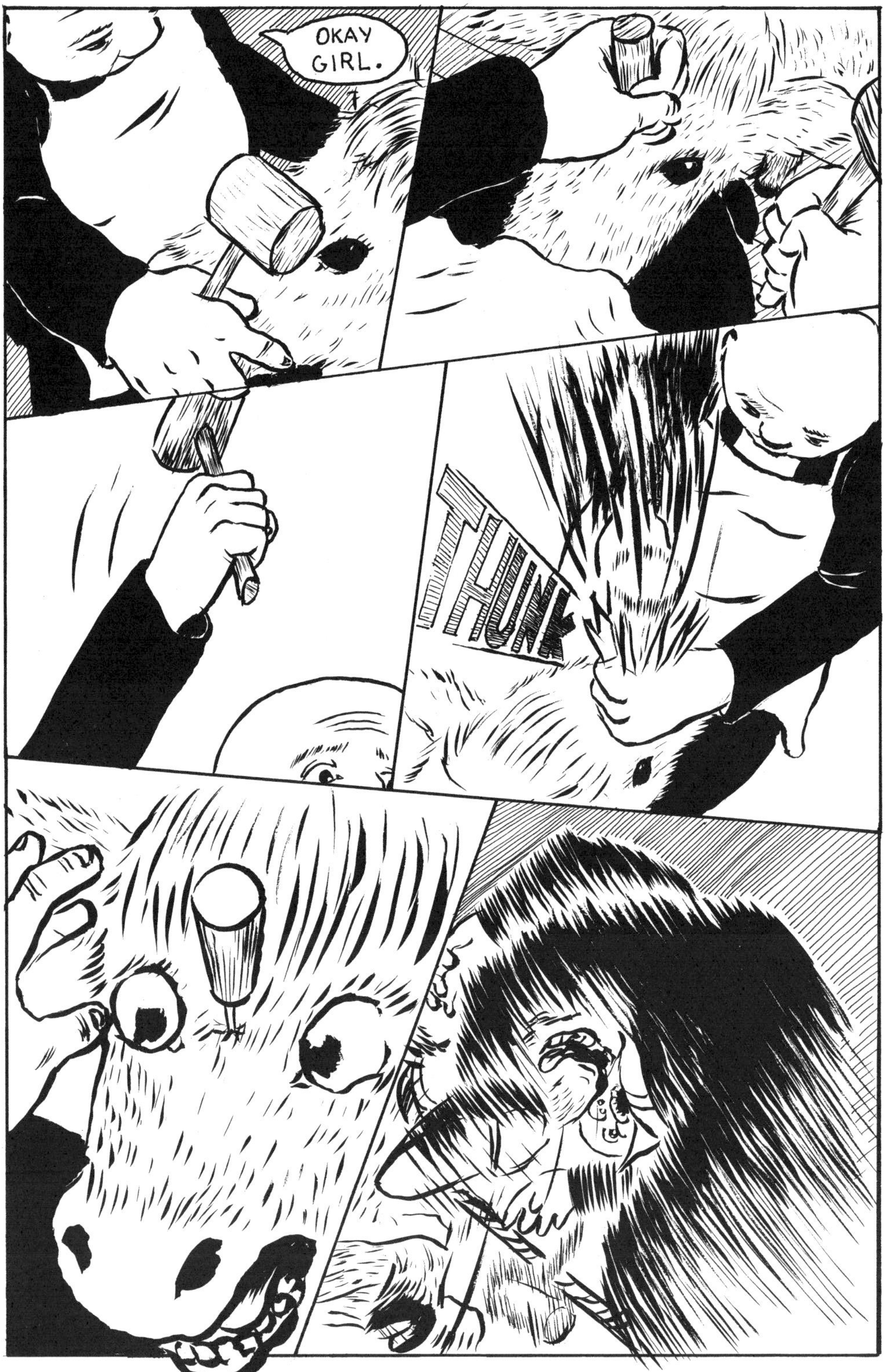
OKAY GIRL.
THUNK

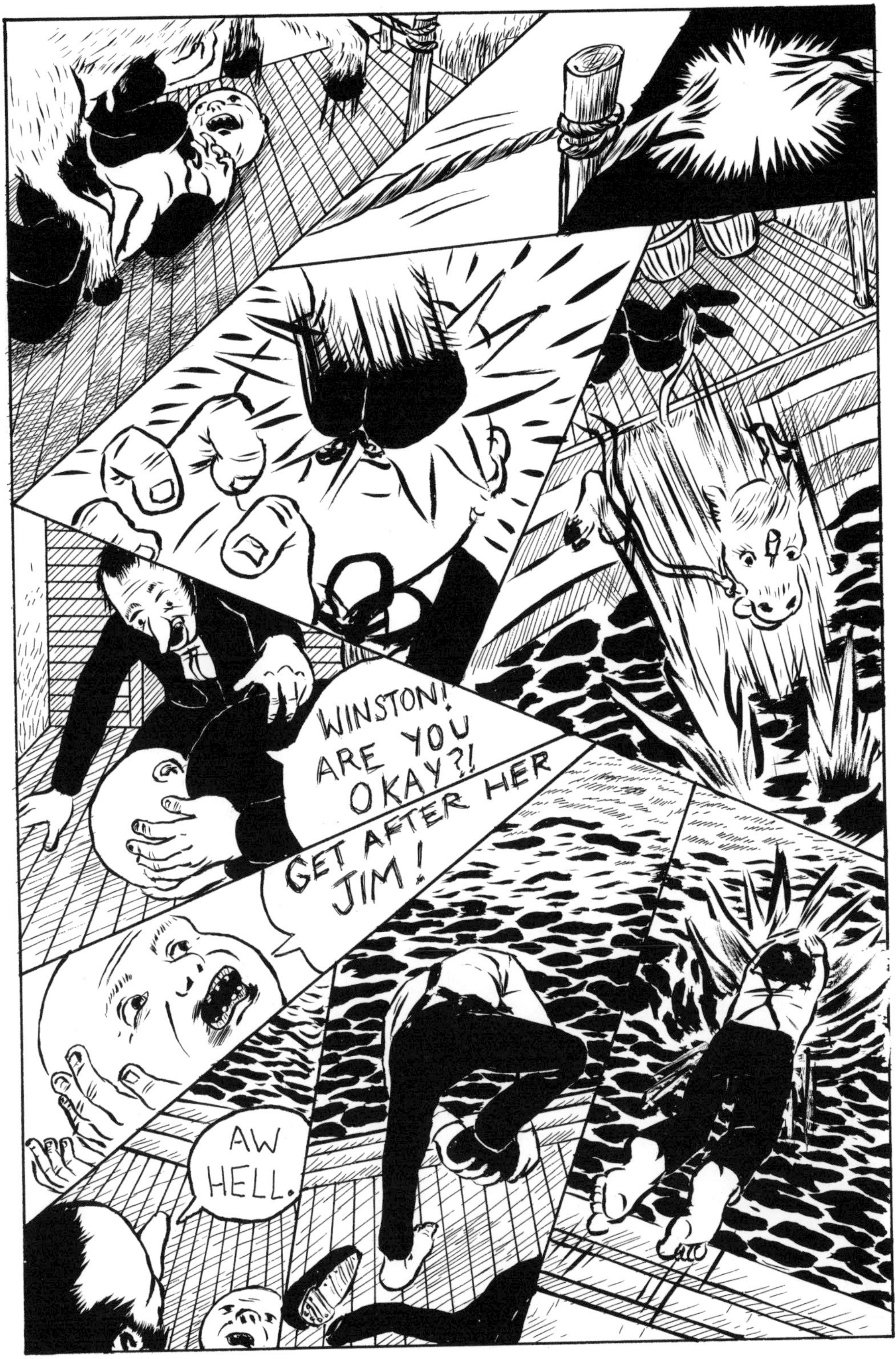
WINSTON! ARE YOU OKAY?!
GET AFTER HER JIM!
AW HELL.

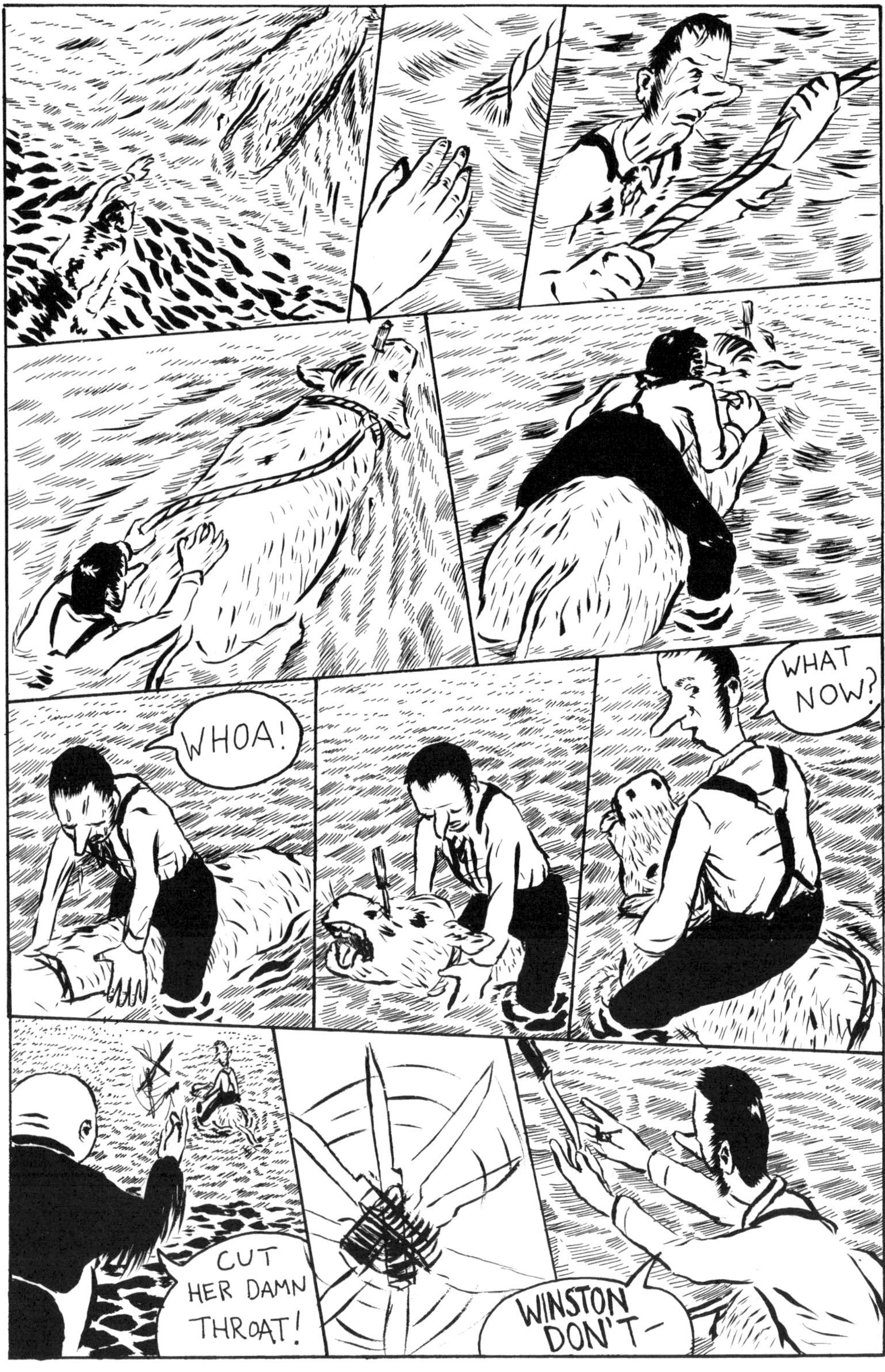
WHOA!
WHAT NOW?
CUT HER DAMN THROAT!
WINSTON DON'T-

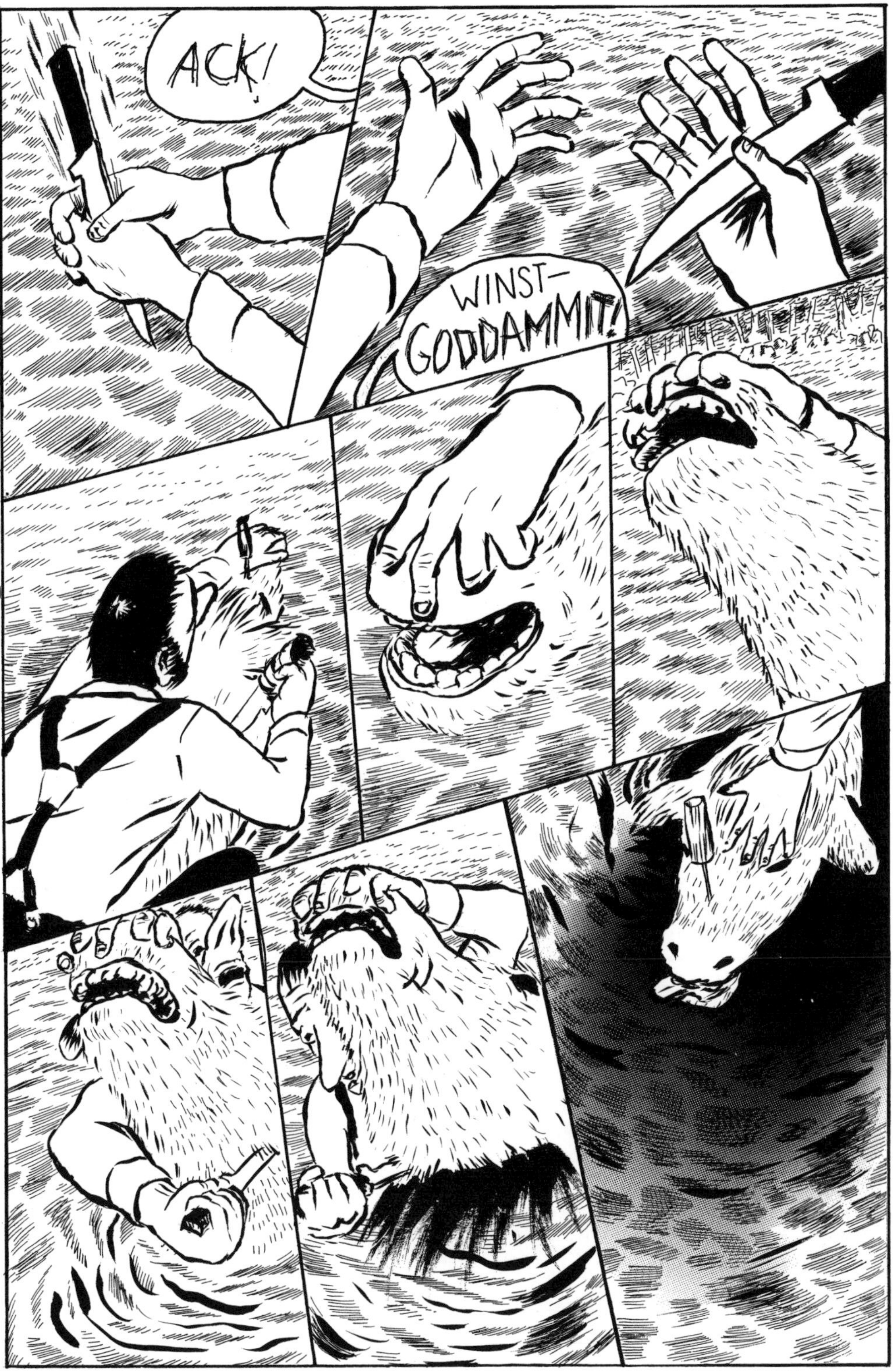
ACK!
WINST-
GODDAMMIT!

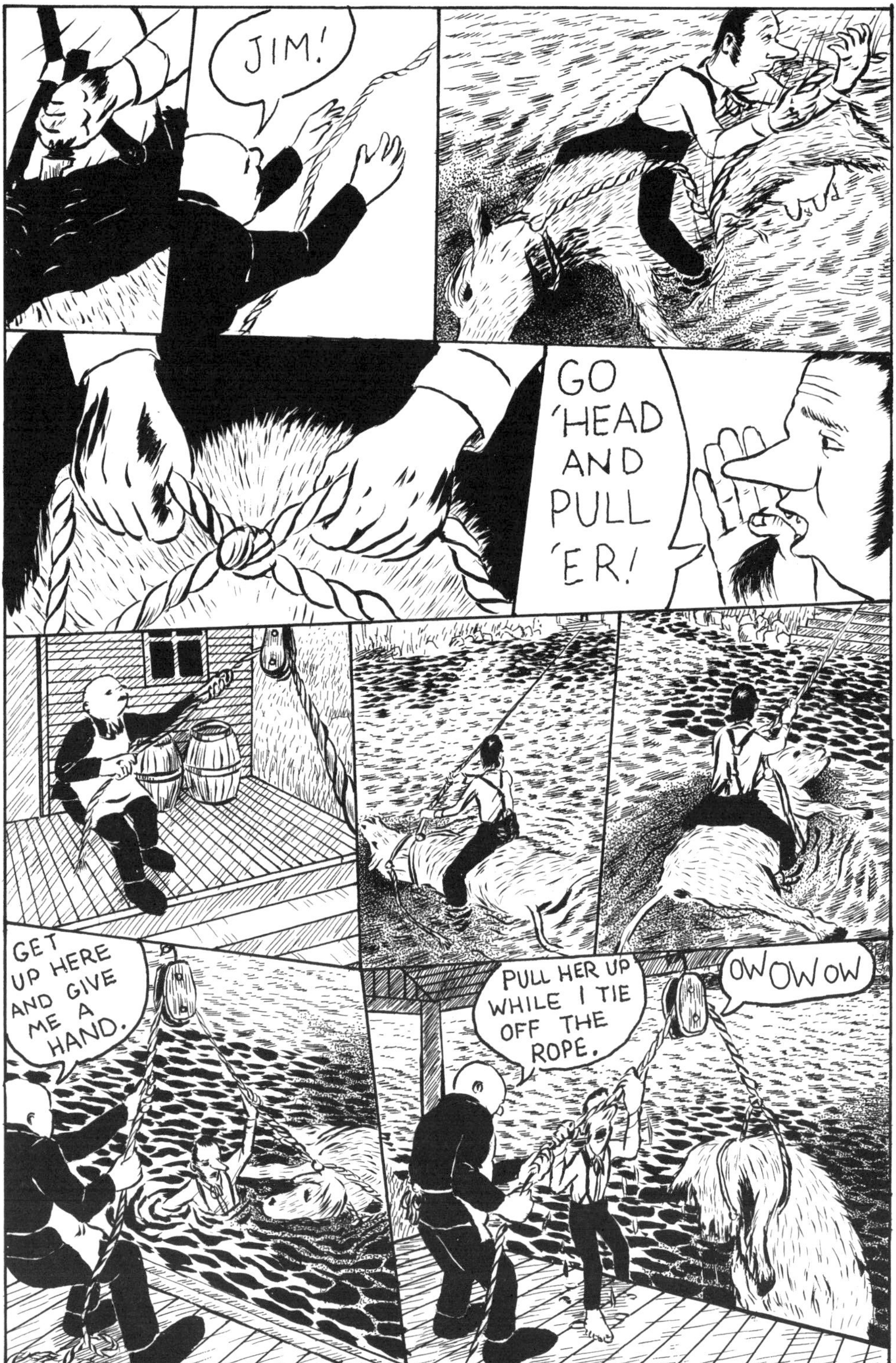

JIM!
GO 'HEAD AND PULL 'ER!
GET UP HERE AND GIVE ME A HAND.
PULL HER UP WHILE I TIE OFF THE ROPE.
OW OW OW OW

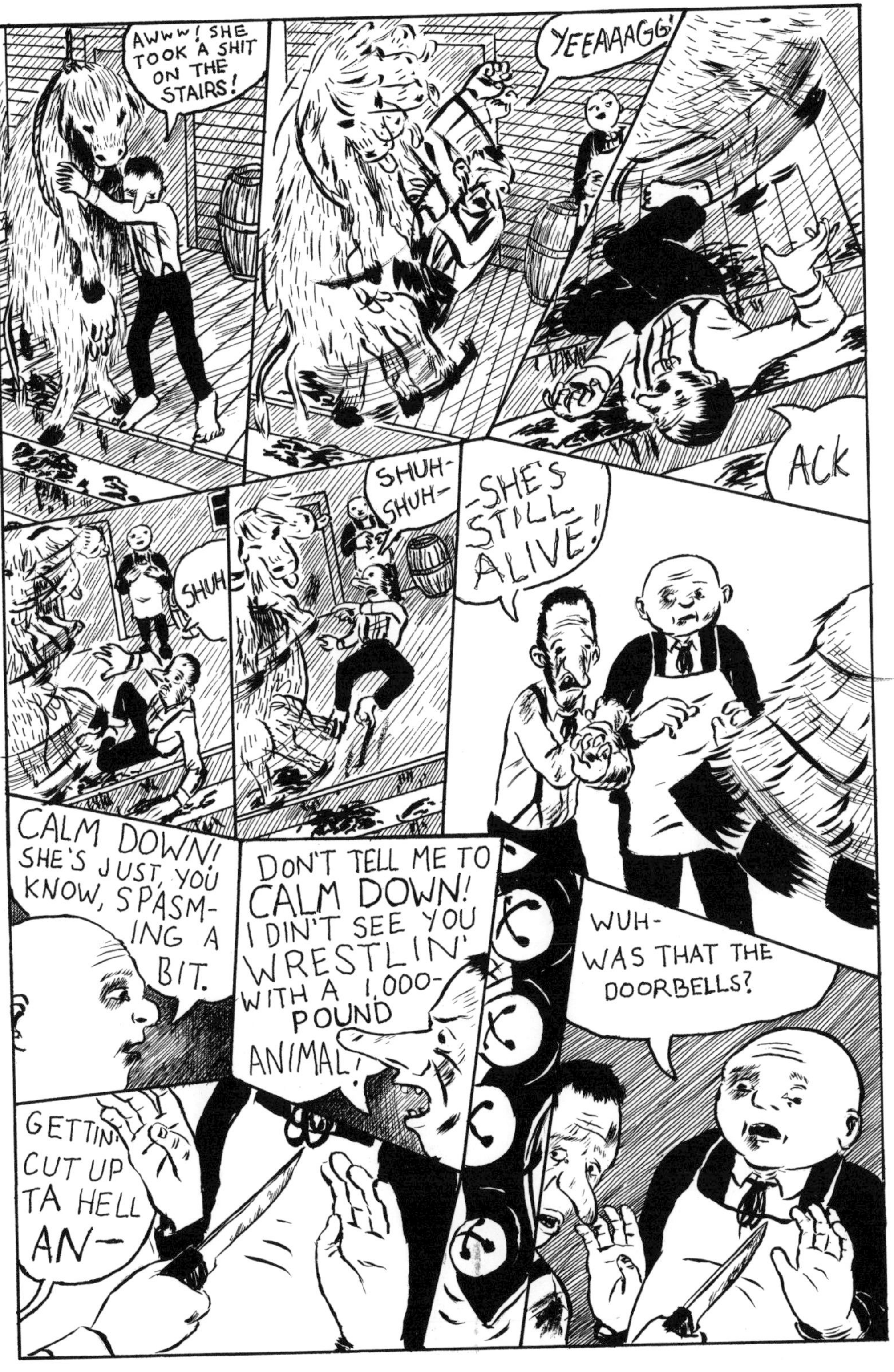
AWWW! SHE TOOK A SHIT ON THE STAIRS!
YEEAAAGG!
ACK
SHUH
SHUH-SHUH-
-SHE'S STILL ALIVE!
CALM DOWN! SHE'S JUST, YOU KNOW, SPASMING A BIT.
DON'T TELL ME TO CALM DOWN! I DIN'T SEE YOU WRESTLIN' WITH A 1,000-POUND ANIMAL!
GETTIN' CUT UP TA HELL AN—
WUH-WAS THAT THE DOORBELLS?

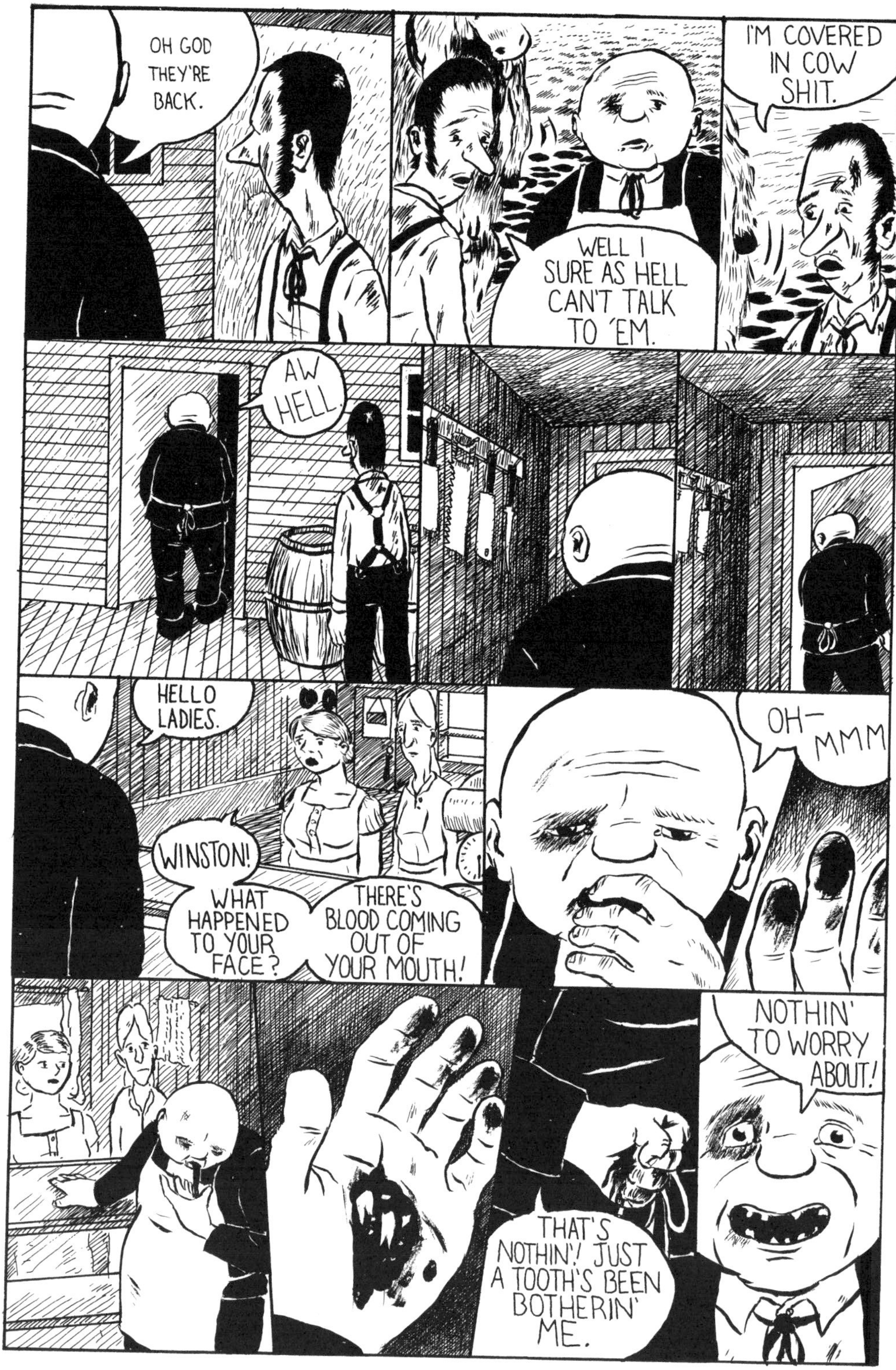
OH GOD THEY'RE BACK.
WELL I SURE AS HELL CAN'T TALK TO 'EM.
I'M COVERED IN COW SHIT.
AW HELL.
HELLO LADIES.
WINSTON!
WHAT HAPPENED TO YOUR FACE?
THERE'S BLOOD COMING OUT OF YOUR MOUTH!
OH-MMM
THAT'S NOTHIN'! JUST A TOOTH'S BEEN BOTHERIN' ME.
NOTHIN' TO WORRY ABOUT!

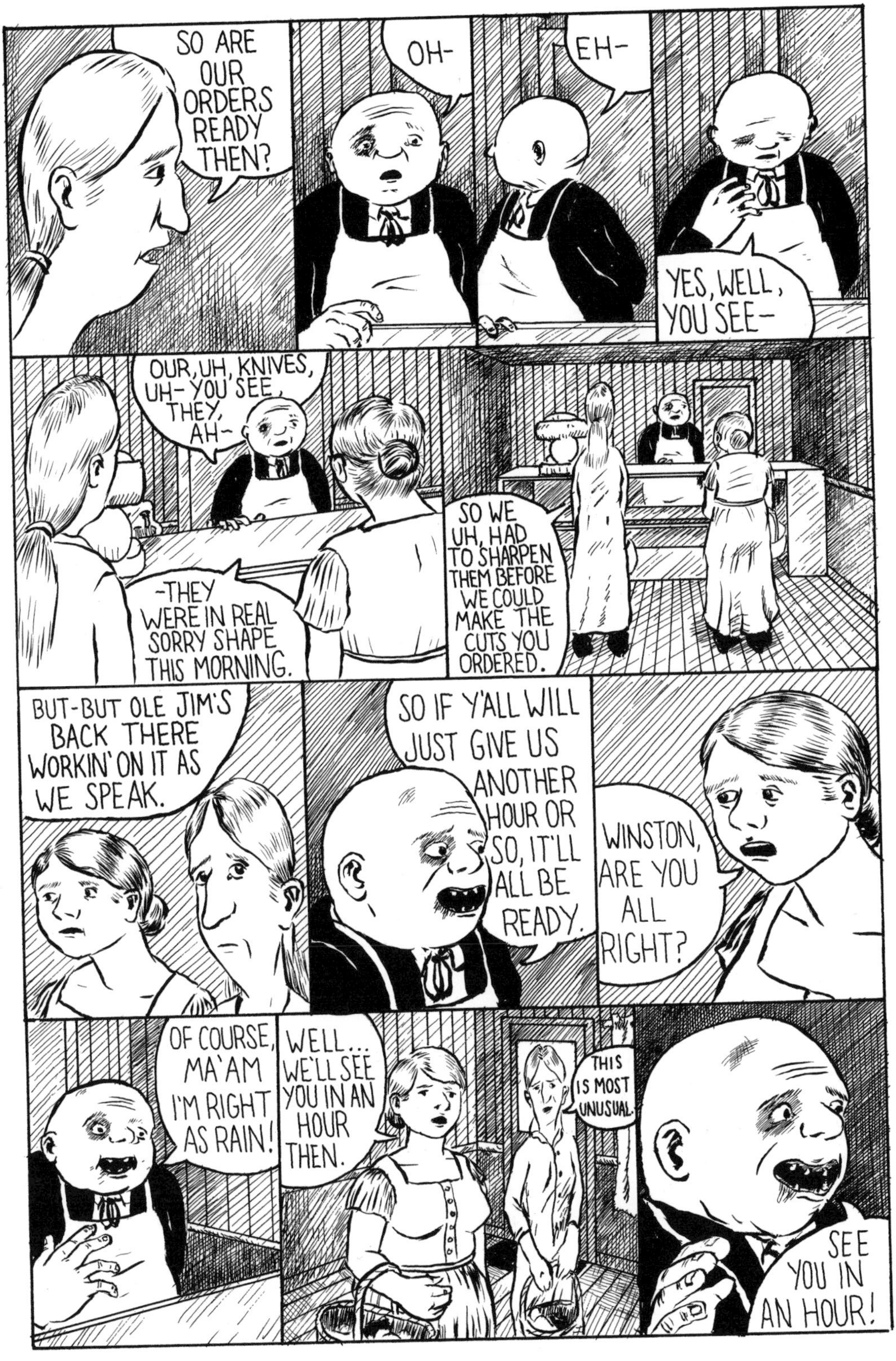
SO ARE OUR ORDERS READY THEN?
OH-
EH-
YES, WELL, YOU SEE-
OUR, UH, KNIVES, UH- YOU SEE, THEY, AH-
-THEY WERE IN REAL SORRY SHAPE THIS MORNING.
SO WE UH, HAD TO SHARPEN THEM BEFORE WE COULD MAKE THE CUTS YOU ORDERED.
BUT-BUT OLE JIM'S BACK THERE WORKIN' ON IT AS WE SPEAK.
SO IF Y'ALL WILL JUST GIVE US ANOTHER HOUR OR SO, IT'LL ALL BE READY.
WINSTON, ARE YOU ALL RIGHT?
OF COURSE, MA'AM I'M RIGHT AS RAIN!
WELL... WE'LL SEE YOU IN AN HOUR THEN.
THIS IS MOST UNUSUAL.
SEE YOU IN AN HOUR!

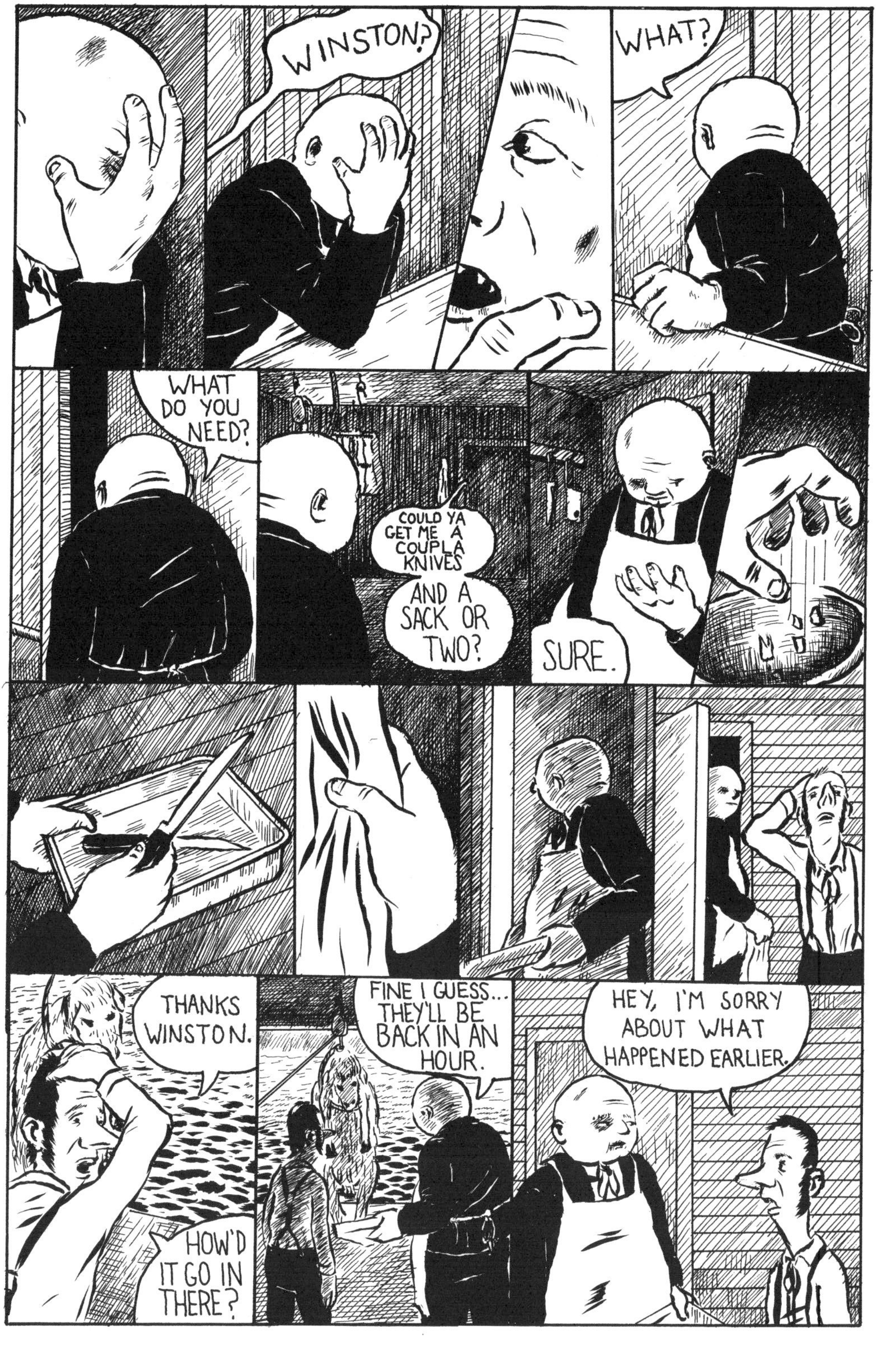
WINSTON?
WHAT?
WHAT DO YOU NEED?
COULD YA GET ME A COUPLA KNIVES
AND A SACK OR TWO?
SURE.
THANKS WINSTON.
HOW'D IT GO IN THERE?
FINE I GUESS... THEY'LL BE BACK IN AN HOUR.
HEY, I'M SORRY ABOUT WHAT HAPPENED EARLIER.

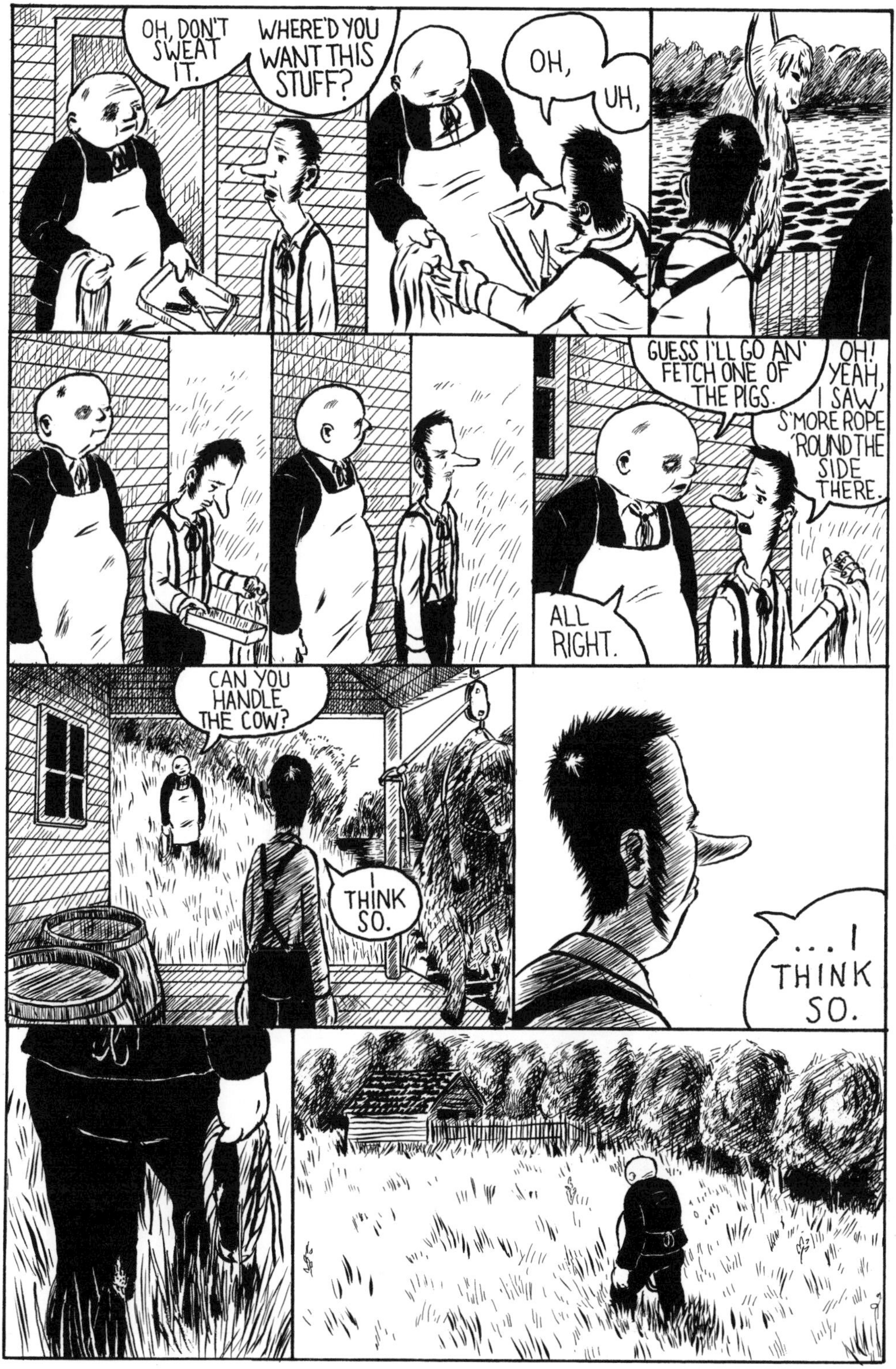
OH, DON'T SWEAT IT.
WHERE'D YOU WANT THIS STUFF?
OH,
UH,
GUESS I'LL GO AN' FETCH ONE OF THE PIGS.
OH! YEAH, I SAW S'MORE ROPE 'ROUND THE SIDE THERE.
ALL RIGHT.
CAN YOU HANDLE THE COW?
I THINK SO.
...I THINK SO.

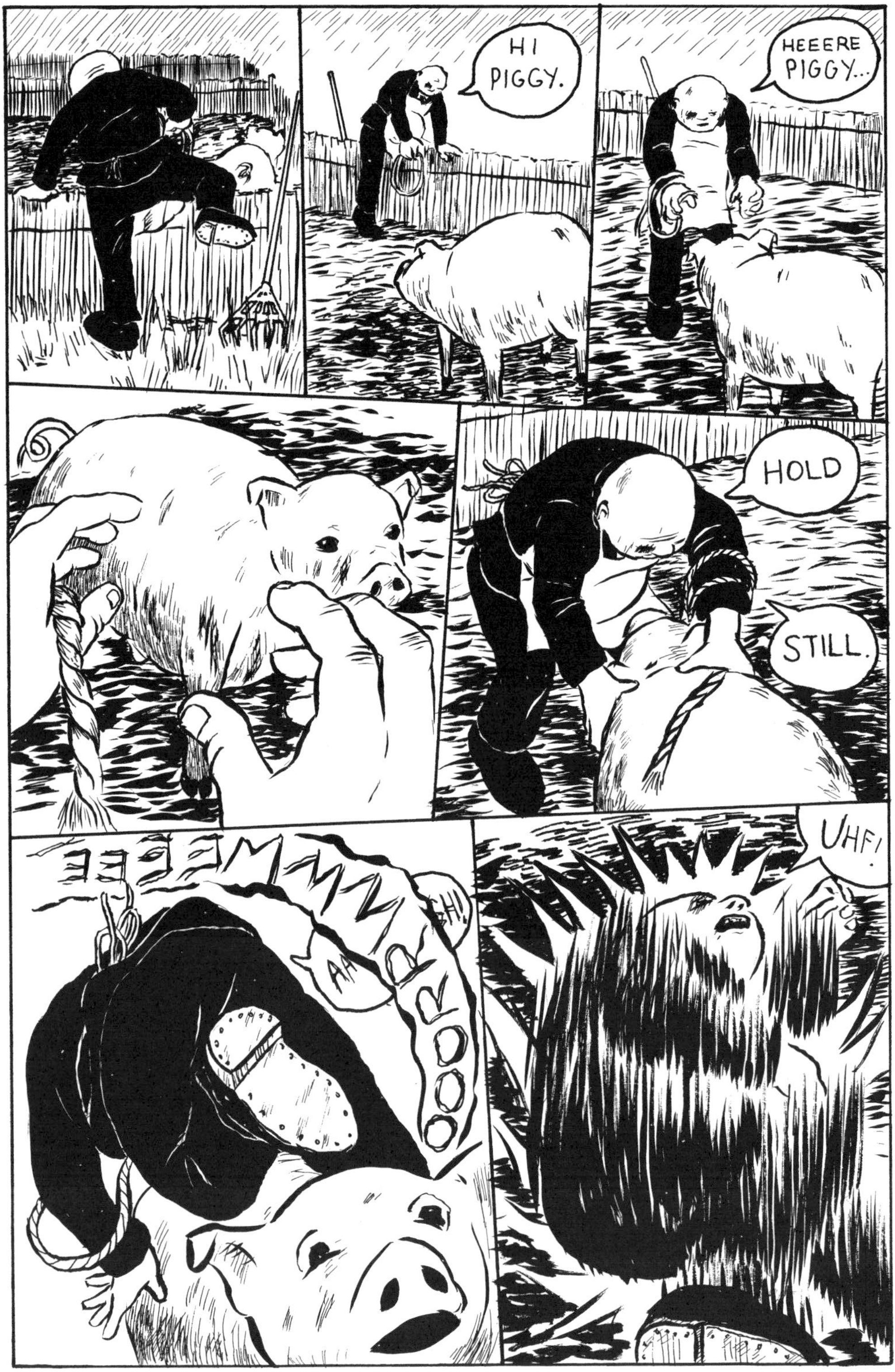

HI PIGGY.
HEEERE PIGGY...
HOLD
STILL.
OOOORRMMMMEEEE
AAGH!
UHF!

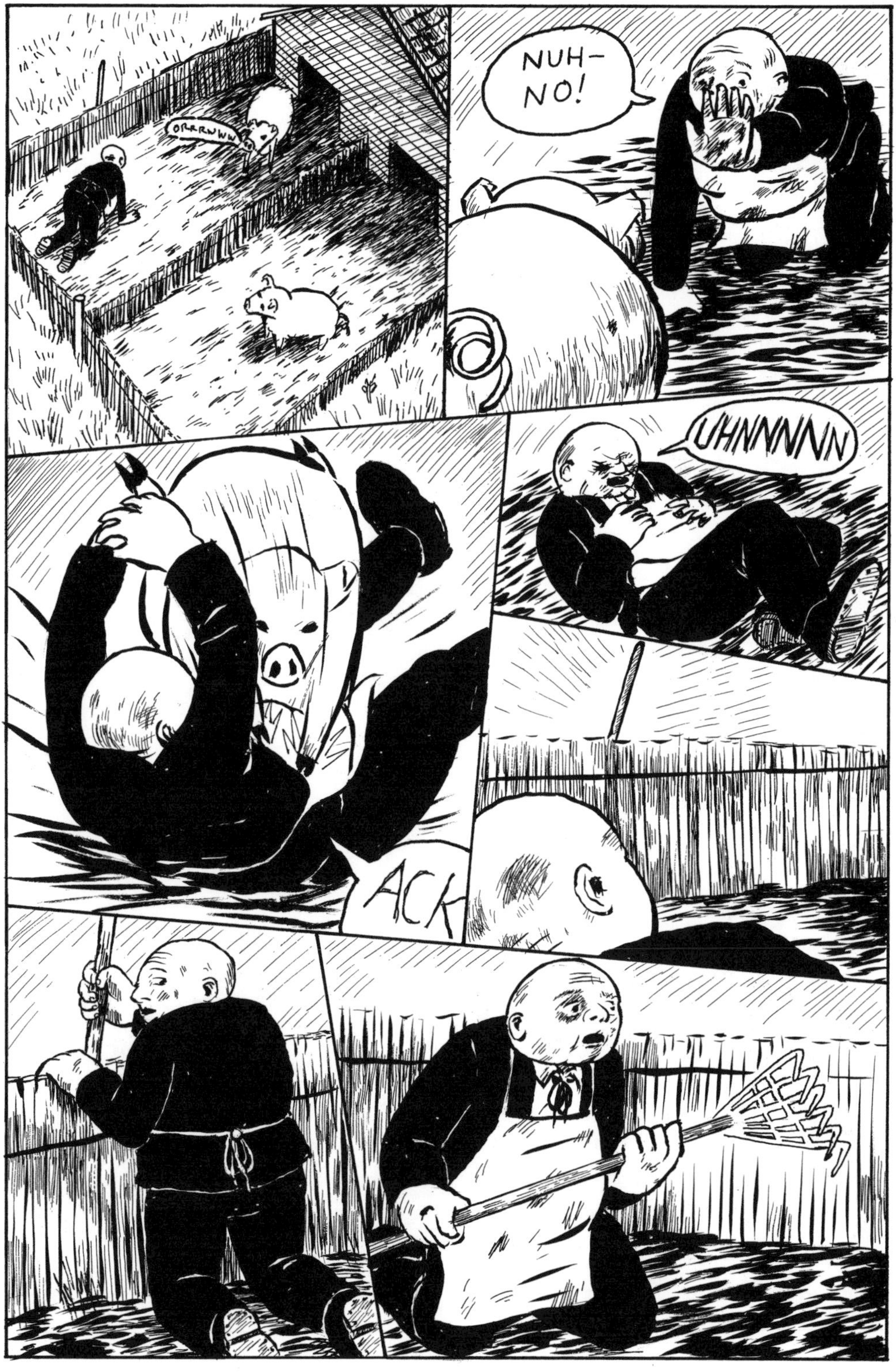
ORRRWWW
NUH-
NO!
UHNNNNN
ACK

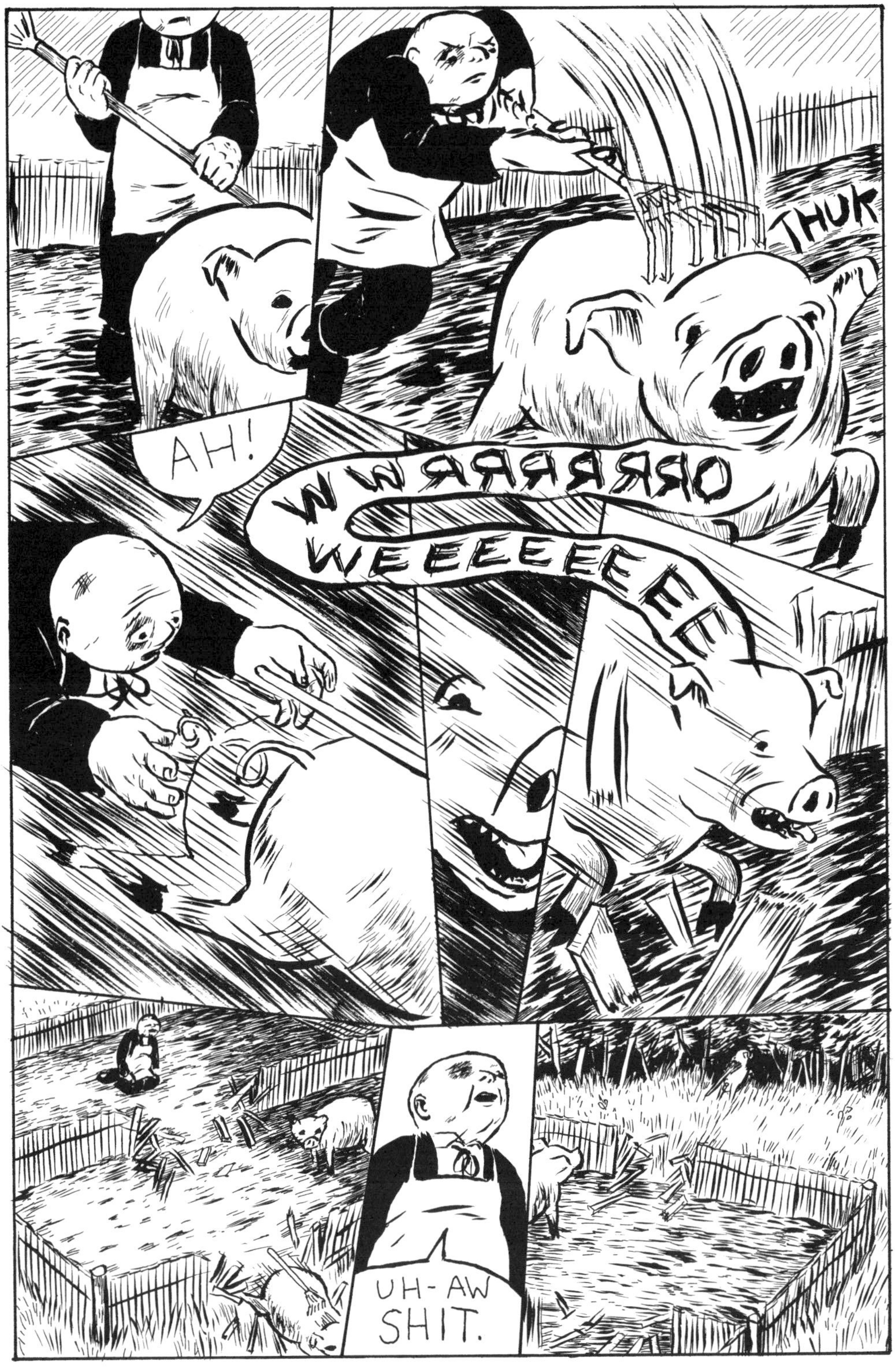
THUK
AH!
ORRRRRWW
WEEEEEEEEE
UH-AW
SHIT.

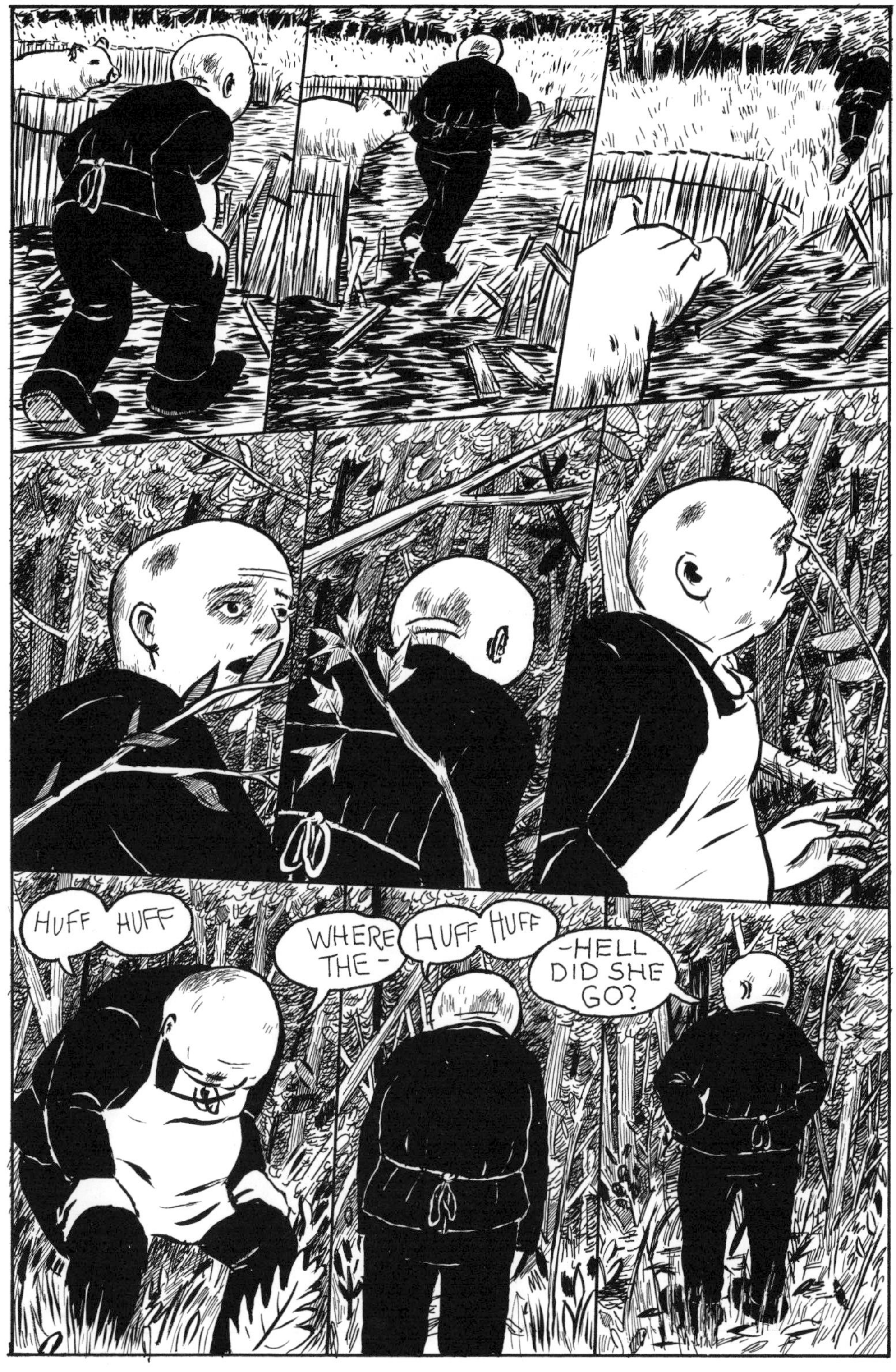
HUFF HUFF
WHERE THE -
HUFF HUFF
-HELL DID SHE GO?

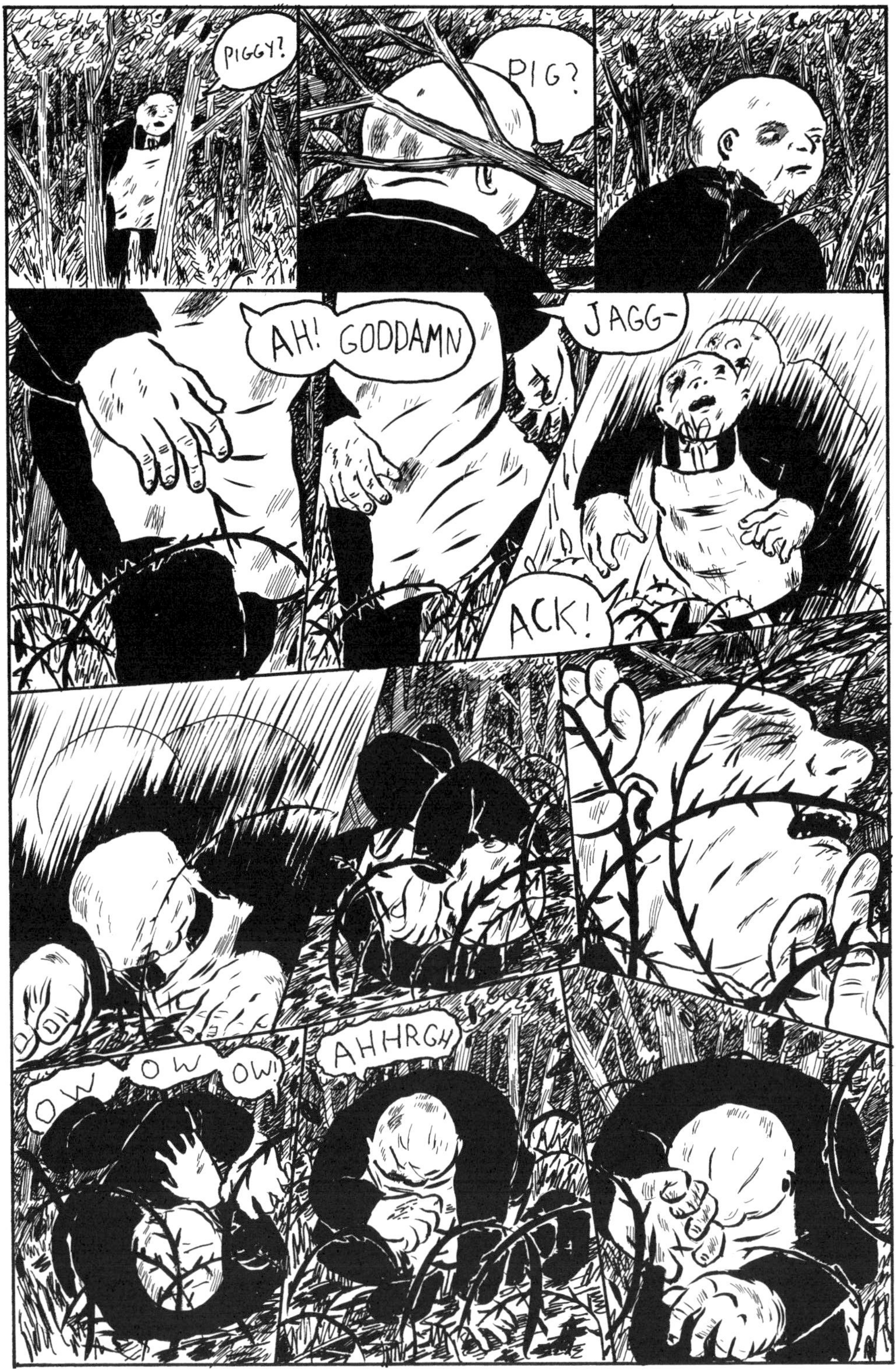
PIGGY?
PIG?
AH!
GODDAMN
JAGG-
ACK!
OW
OW
OW!
AHHRGH

OCTOBER 19, XXXX

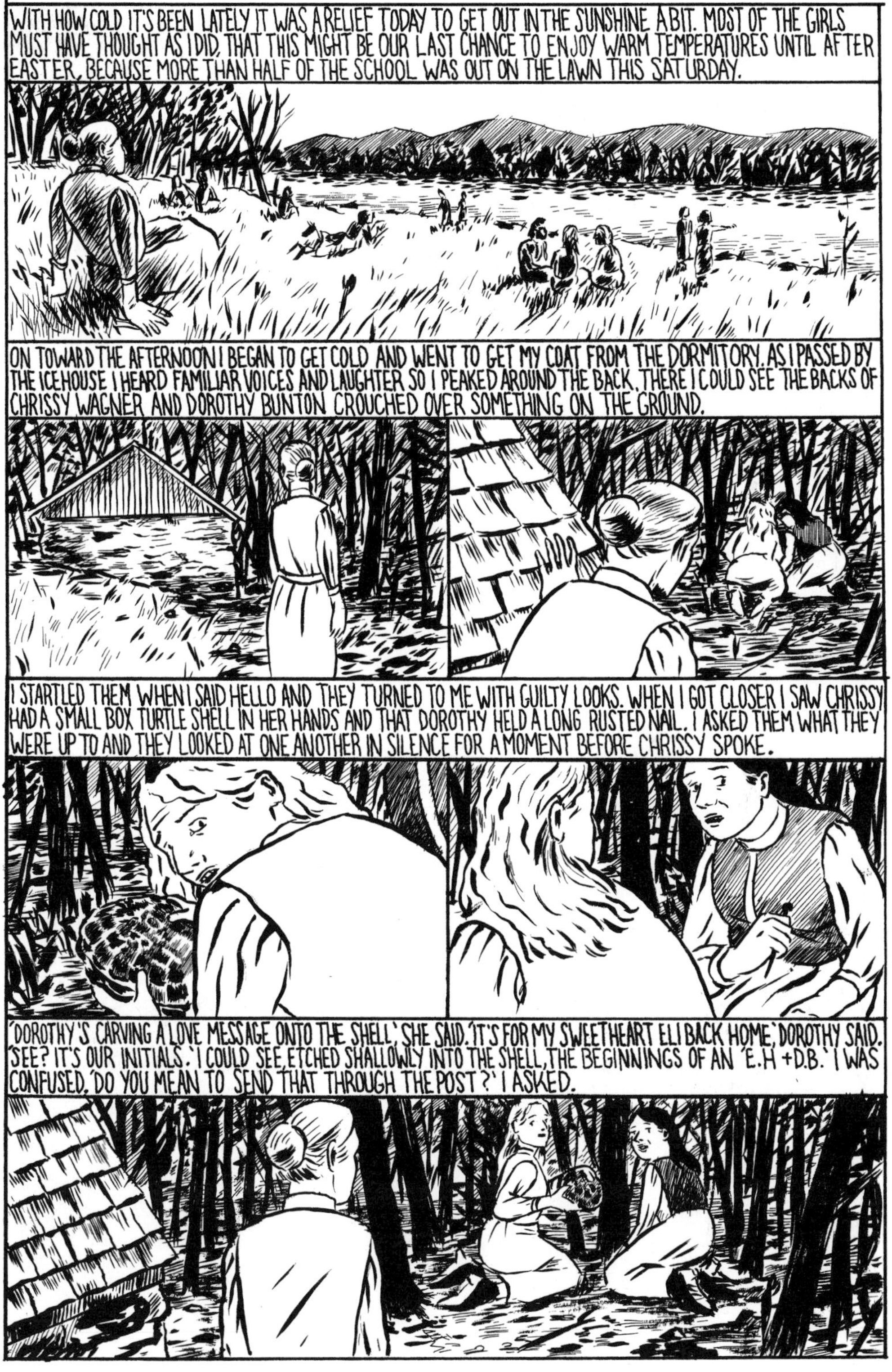
WITH HOW COLD IT'S BEEN LATELY IT WAS A RELIEF TODAY TO GET OUT IN THE SUNSHINE A BIT. MOST OF THE GIRLS MUST HAVE THOUGHT AS I DID, THAT THIS MIGHT BE OUR LAST CHANCE TO ENJOY WARM TEMPERATURES UNTIL AFTER EASTER, BECAUSE MORE THAN HALF OF THE SCHOOL WAS OUT ON THE LAWN THIS SATURDAY.
ON TOWARD THE AFTERNOON I BEGAN TO GET COLD AND WENT TO GET MY COAT FROM THE DORMITORY. AS I PASSED BY THE ICEHOUSE I HEARD FAMILIAR VOICES AND LAUGHTER SO I PEAKED AROUND THE BACK. THERE I COULD SEE THE BACKS OF CHRISSY WAGNER AND DOROTHY BUNTON CROUCHED OVER SOMETHING ON THE GROUND.
I STARTLED THEM WHEN I SAID HELLO AND THEY TURNED TO ME WITH GUILTY LOOKS. WHEN I GOT CLOSER I SAW CHRISSY HAD A SMALL BOX TURTLE SHELL IN HER HANDS AND THAT DOROTHY HELD A LONG RUSTED NAIL. I ASKED THEM WHAT THEY WERE UP TO AND THEY LOOKED AT ONE ANOTHER IN SILENCE FOR A MOMENT BEFORE CHRISSY SPOKE.
'DOROTHY'S CARVING A LOVE MESSAGE ONTO THE SHELL,' SHE SAID. 'IT'S FOR MY SWEETHEART ELI BACK HOME,' DOROTHY SAID. 'SEE? IT'S OUR INITIALS.' I COULD SEE, ETCHED SHALLOWLY INTO THE SHELL, THE BEGINNINGS OF AN 'E.H + D.B.' I WAS CONFUSED. 'DO YOU MEAN TO SEND THAT THROUGH THE POST?' I ASKED.

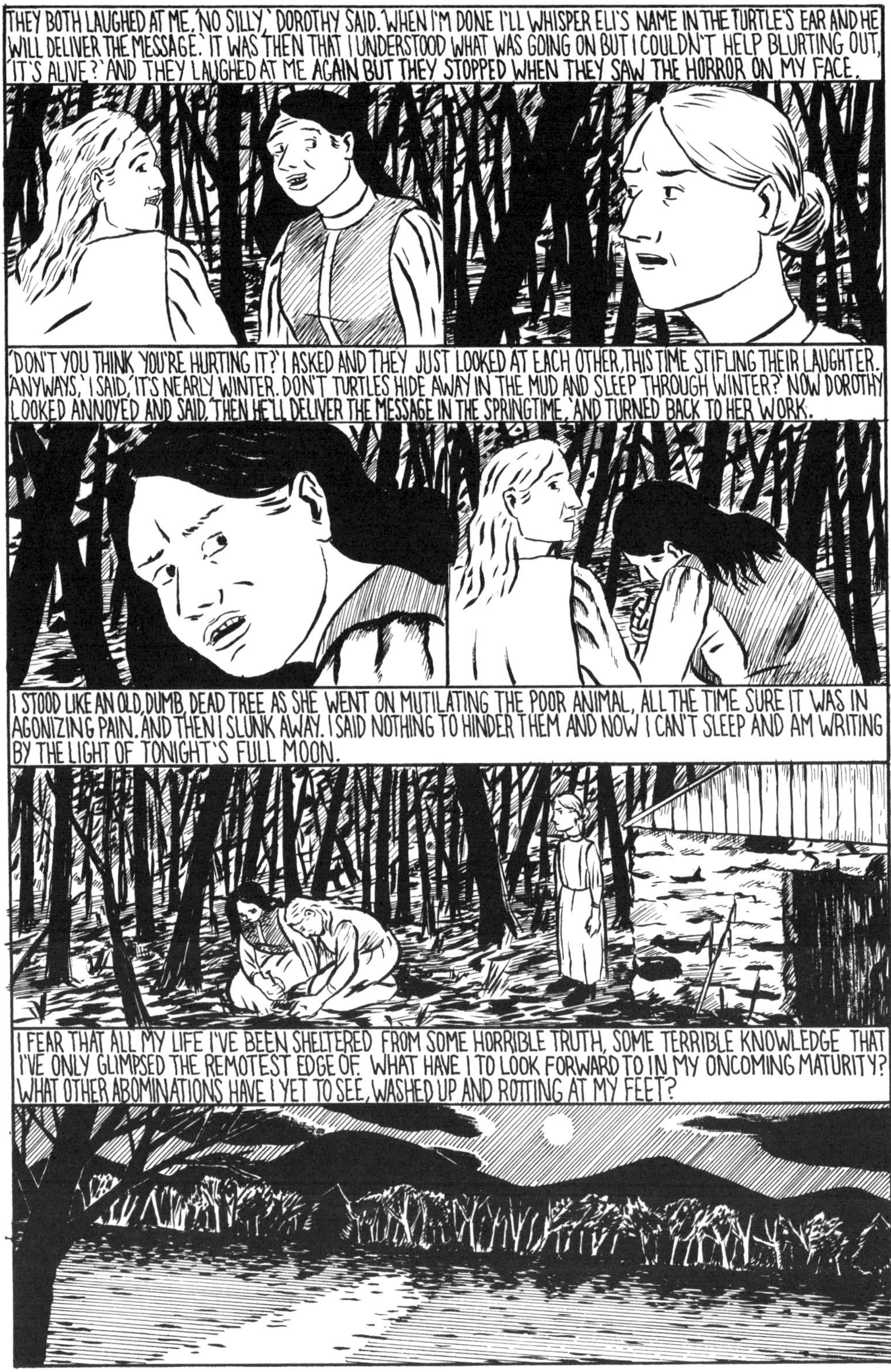
THEY BOTH LAUGHED AT ME. 'NO SILLY,' DOROTHY SAID. 'WHEN I'M DONE I'LL WHISPER ELI'S NAME IN THE TURTLE'S EAR AND HE WILL DELIVER THE MESSAGE.' IT WAS THEN THAT I UNDERSTOOD WHAT WAS GOING ON BUT I COULDN'T HELP BLURTING OUT, 'IT'S ALIVE?' AND THEY LAUGHED AT ME AGAIN BUT THEY STOPPED WHEN THEY SAW THE HORROR ON MY FACE.
'DON'T YOU THINK YOU'RE HURTING IT?' I ASKED AND THEY JUST LOOKED AT EACH OTHER, THIS TIME STIFLING THEIR LAUGHTER. 'ANYWAYS,' I SAID, 'IT'S NEARLY WINTER. DON'T TURTLES HIDE AWAY IN THE MUD AND SLEEP THROUGH WINTER?' NOW DOROTHY LOOKED ANNOYED AND SAID, 'THEN HE'LL DELIVER THE MESSAGE IN THE SPRINGTIME,' AND TURNED BACK TO HER WORK.
I STOOD LIKE AN OLD, DUMB, DEAD TREE AS SHE WENT ON MUTILATING THE POOR ANIMAL, ALL THE TIME SURE IT WAS IN AGONIZING PAIN. AND THEN I SLUNK AWAY. I SAID NOTHING TO HINDER THEM AND NOW I CAN'T SLEEP AND AM WRITING BY THE LIGHT OF TONIGHT'S FULL MOON.
I FEAR THAT ALL MY LIFE I'VE BEEN SHELTERED FROM SOME HORRIBLE TRUTH, SOME TERRIBLE KNOWLEDGE THAT I'VE ONLY GLIMPSED THE REMOTEST EDGE OF. WHAT HAVE I TO LOOK FORWARD TO IN MY ONCOMING MATURITY? WHAT OTHER ABOMINATIONS HAVE I YET TO SEE, WASHED UP AND ROTTING AT MY FEET?

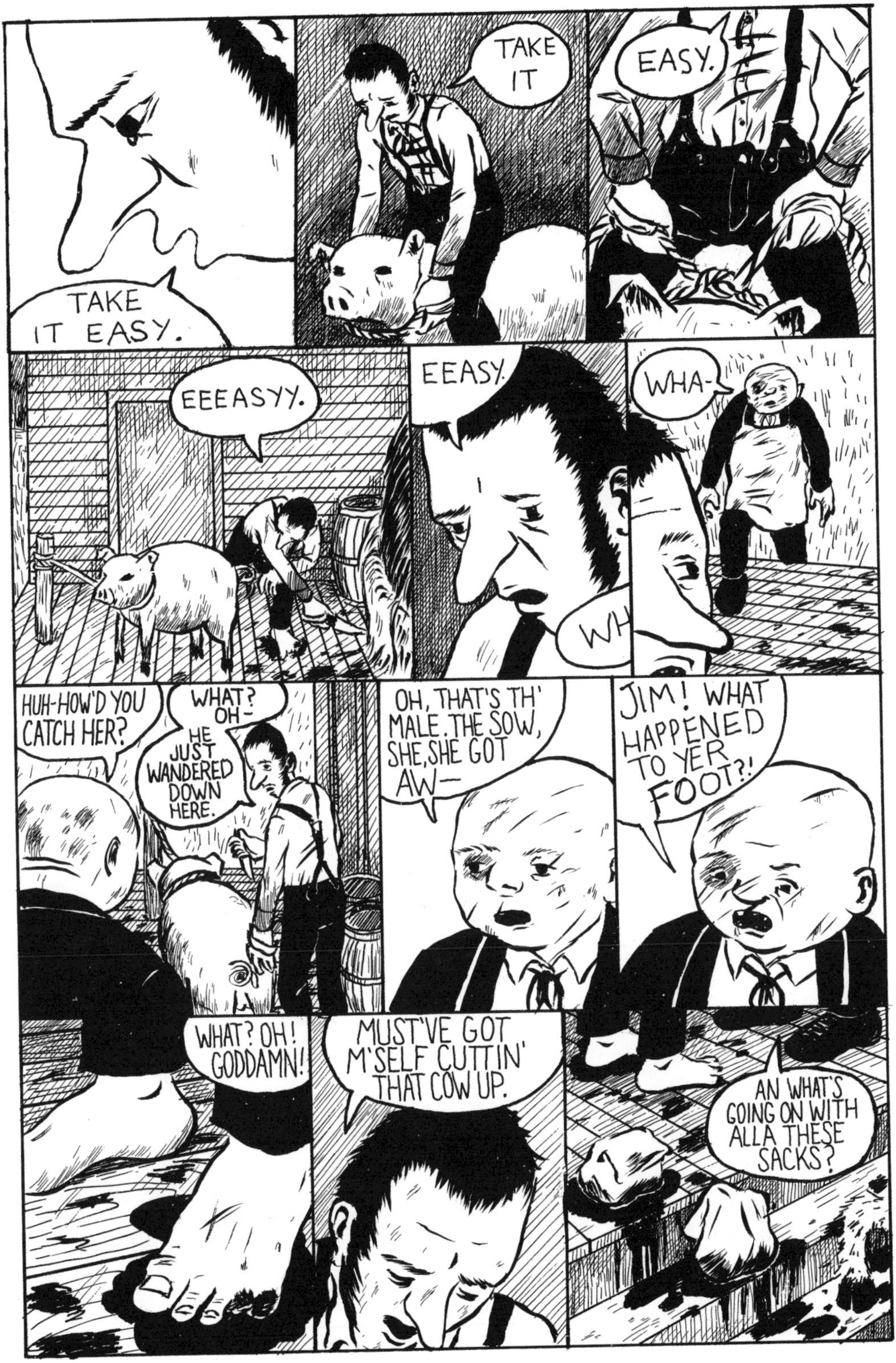
TAKE IT EASY.
TAKE IT
EASY.
EEEASYY.
EEASY.
WHA-
WH
HUH-HOW'D YOU CATCH HER?
WHAT? OH-
HE JUST WANDERED DOWN HERE.
OH, THAT'S TH' MALE. THE SOW, SHE, SHE GOT AW—
JIM! WHAT HAPPENED TO YER FOOT?!
WHAT? OH! GODDAMN!
MUST'VE GOT M'SELF CUTTIN' THAT COW UP.
AN WHAT'S GOING ON WITH ALLA THESE SACKS?

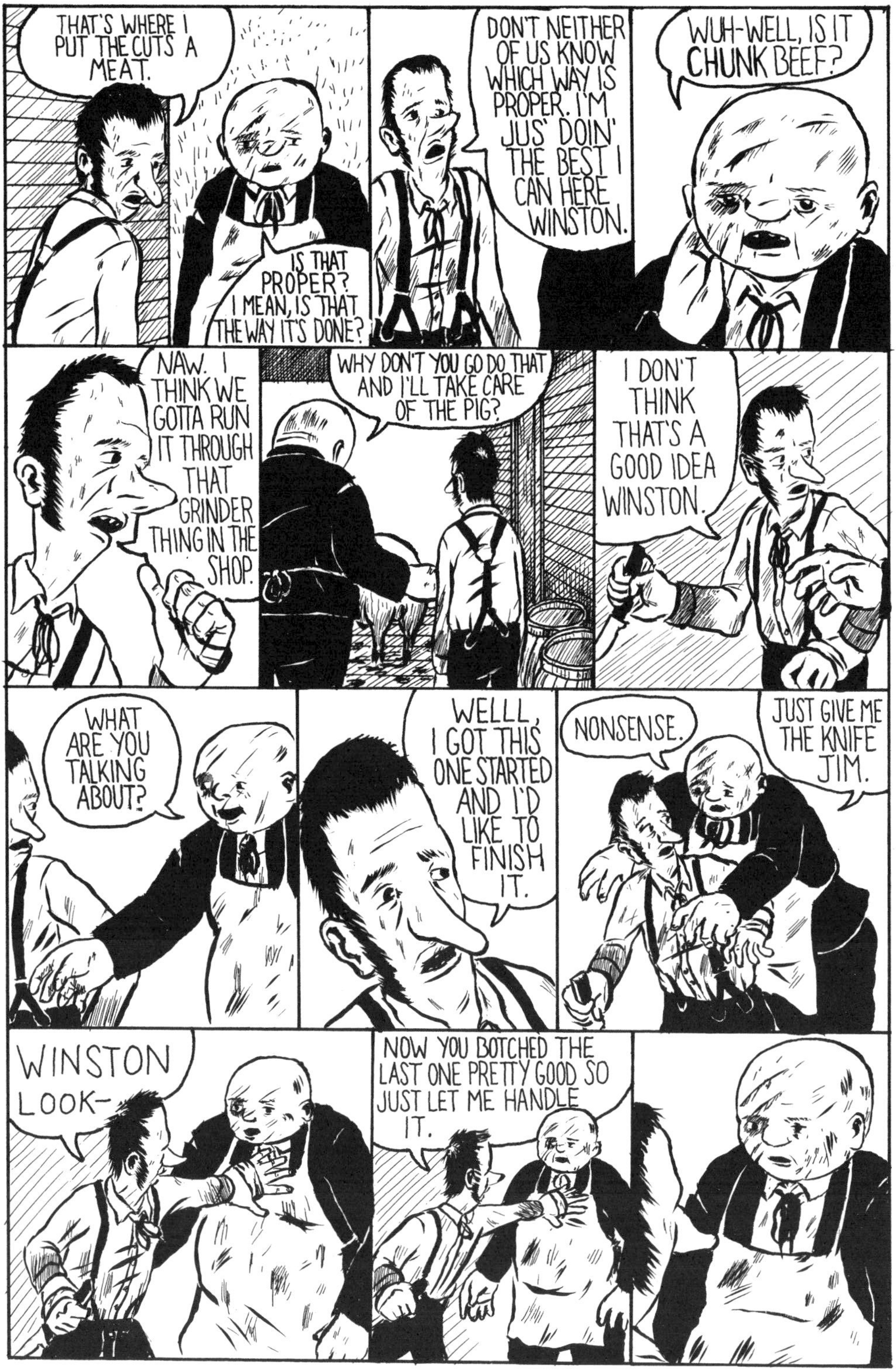
THAT'S WHERE I PUT THE CUTS A MEAT.
IS THAT PROPER? I MEAN, IS THAT THE WAY IT'S DONE?
DON'T NEITHER OF US KNOW WHICH WAY IS PROPER. I'M JUS' DOIN' THE BEST I CAN HERE WINSTON.
WUH-WELL, IS IT CHUNK BEEF?
NAW. I THINK WE GOTTA RUN IT THROUGH THAT GRINDER THING IN THE SHOP.
WHY DON'T YOU GO DO THAT AND I'LL TAKE CARE OF THE PIG?
I DON'T THINK THAT'S A GOOD IDEA WINSTON.
WHAT ARE YOU TALKING ABOUT?
WELLL, I GOT THIS ONE STARTED AND I'D LIKE TO FINISH IT.
NONSENSE.
JUST GIVE ME THE KNIFE JIM.
WINSTON LOOK-
NOW YOU BOTCHED THE LAST ONE PRETTY GOOD SO JUST LET ME HANDLE IT.

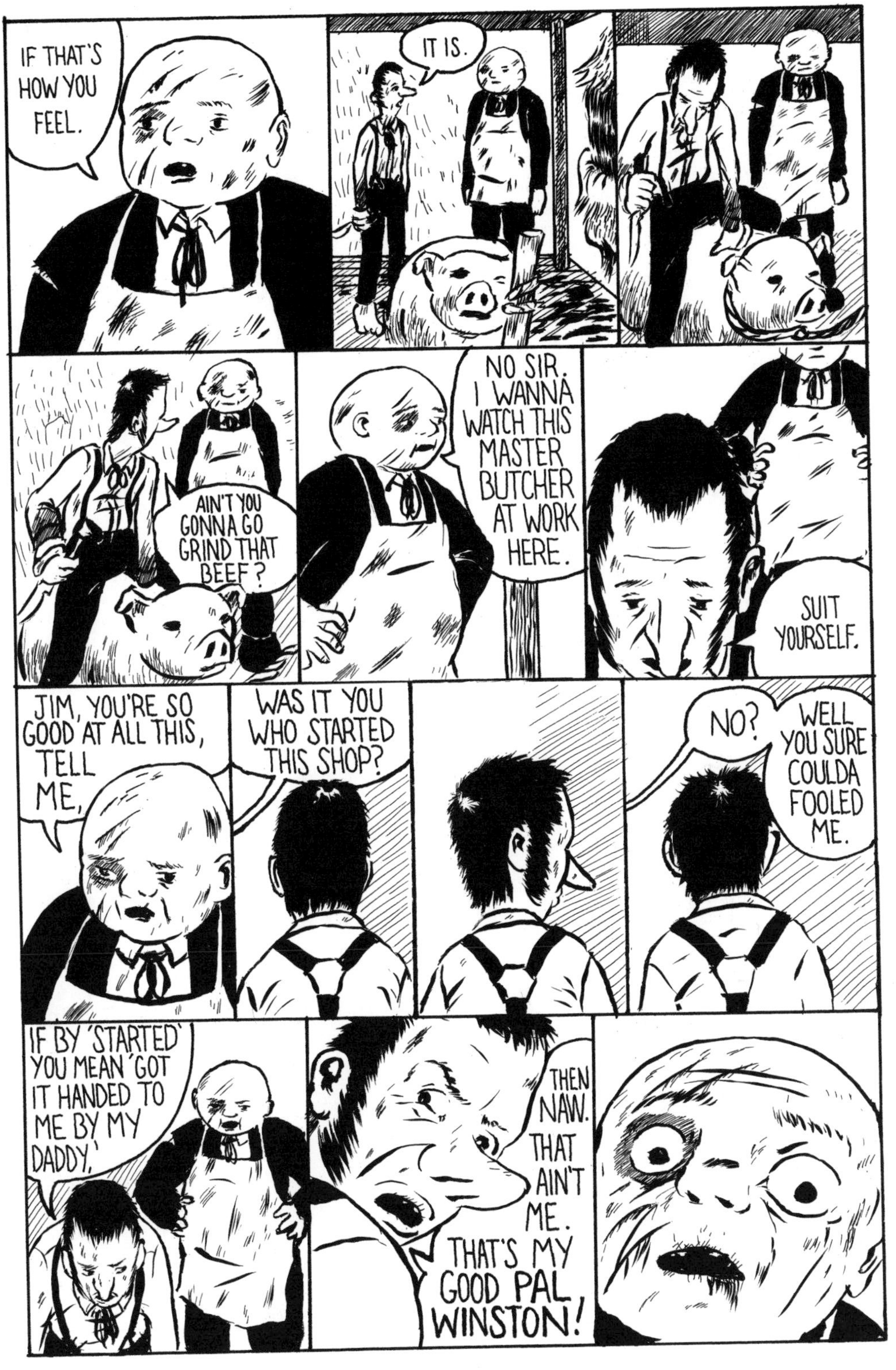
IF THAT'S HOW YOU FEEL.
IT IS.
AIN'T YOU GONNA GO GRIND THAT BEEF?
NO SIR. I WANNA WATCH THIS MASTER BUTCHER AT WORK HERE.
SUIT YOURSELF.
JIM, YOU'RE SO GOOD AT ALL THIS, TELL ME,
WAS IT YOU WHO STARTED THIS SHOP?
NO?
WELL YOU SURE COULDA FOOLED ME.
IF BY 'STARTED' YOU MEAN 'GOT IT HANDED TO ME BY MY DADDY,'
THEN NAW. THAT AIN'T ME.
THAT'S MY GOOD PAL WINSTON!

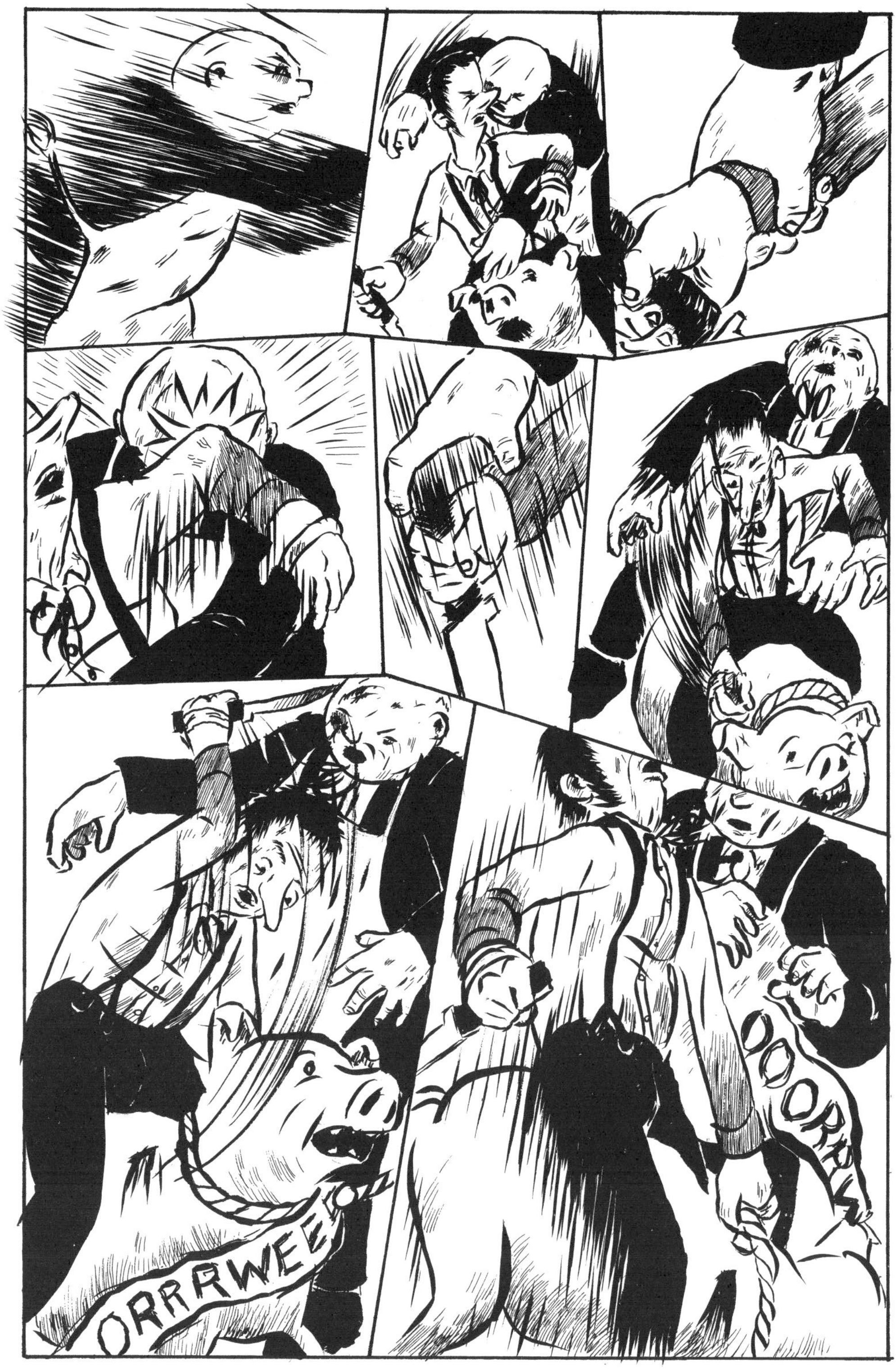
ORRRWEE
OOORRRW

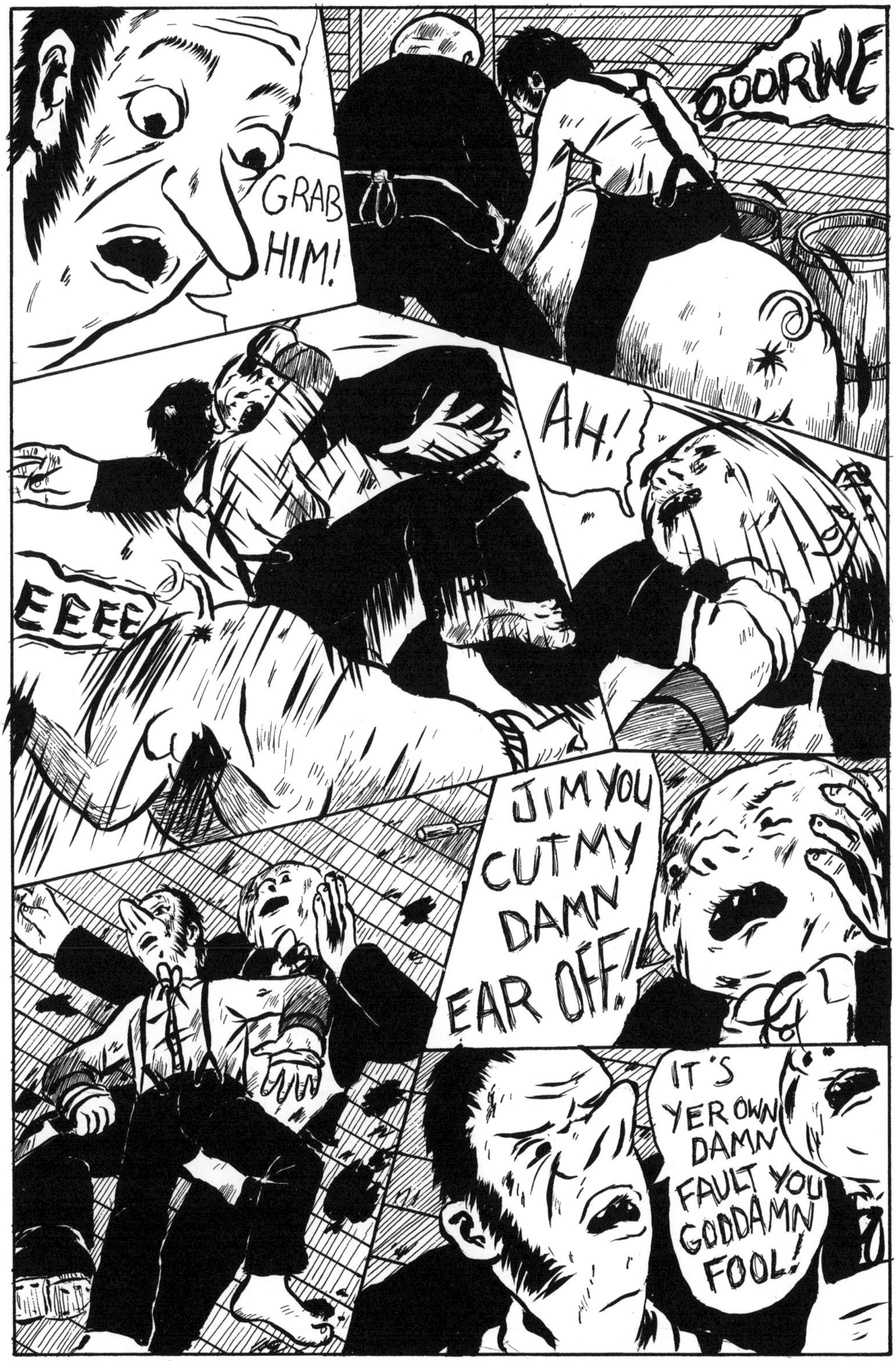
GRAB HIM!
OOORWE
AH!
EEEE
JIM YOU CUT MY DAMN EAR OFF!
IT'S YER OWN DAMN FAULT YOU GODDAMN FOOL!

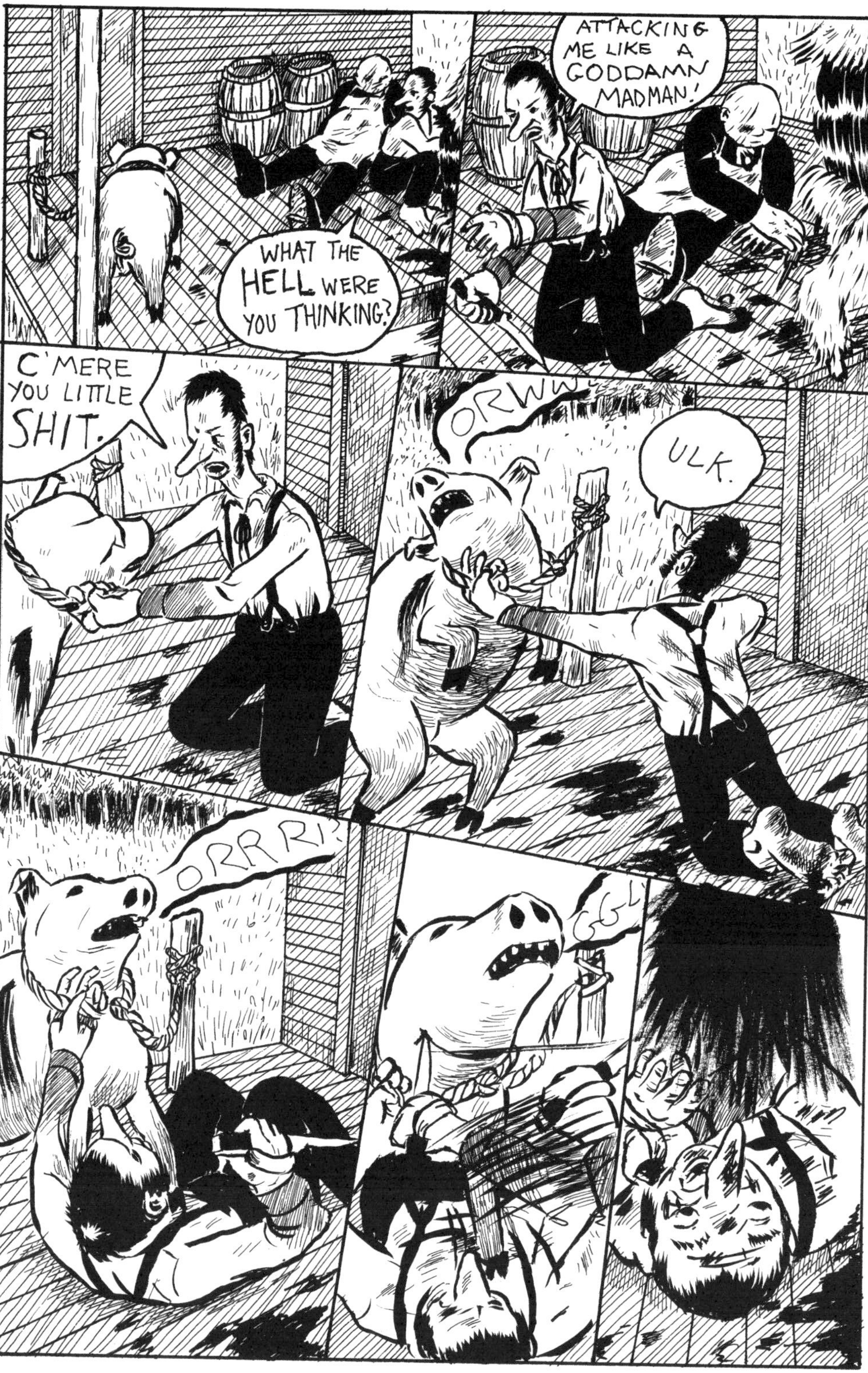
WHAT THE HELL WERE YOU THINKING?
ATTACKING ME LIKE A GODDAMN MADMAN!
C'MERE YOU LITTLE SHIT.
ORWW
ULK.
ORRRR

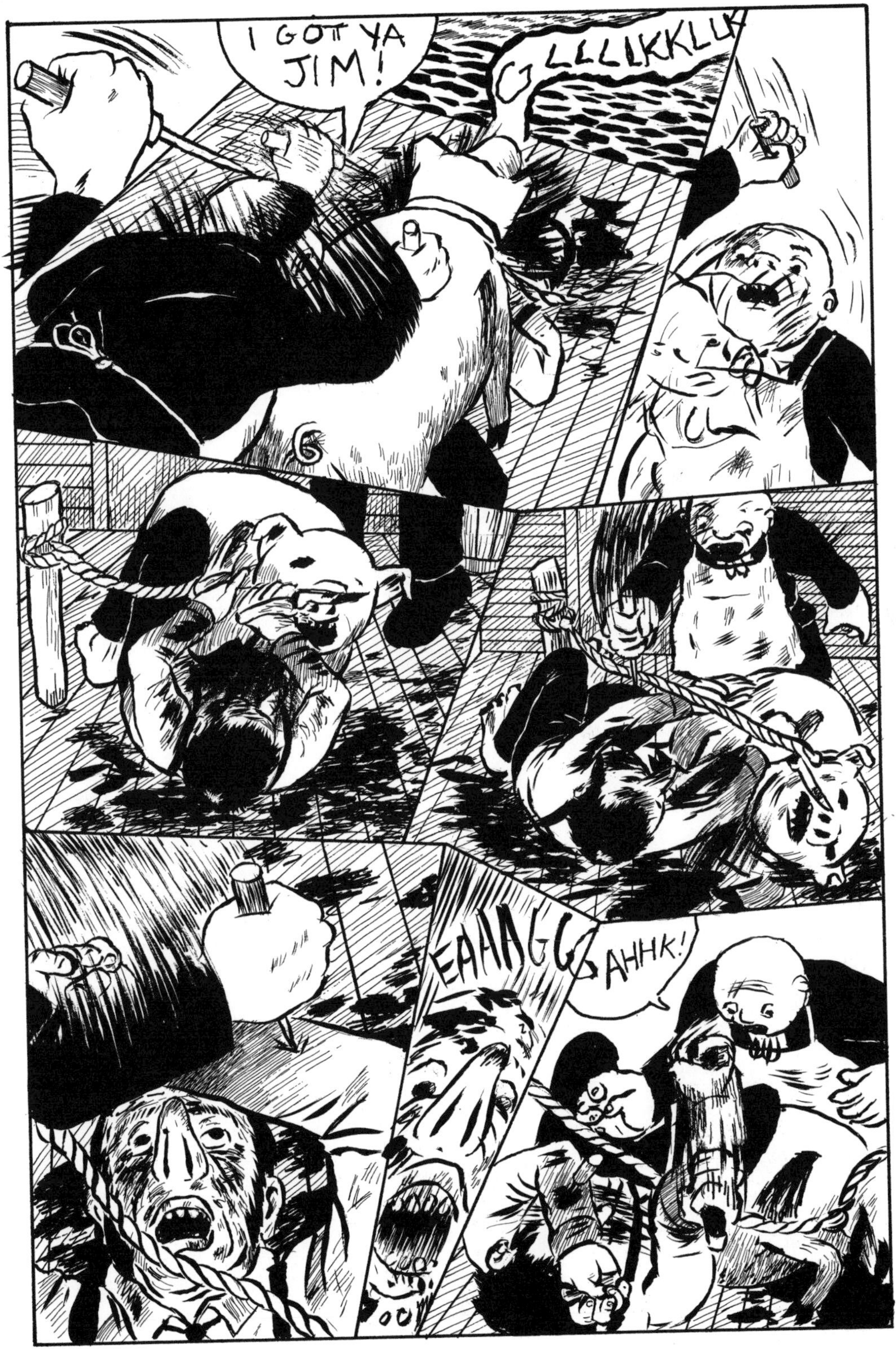
I GOT YA JIM!
GLLLLKKLLK
EAAAGG
AHHK!

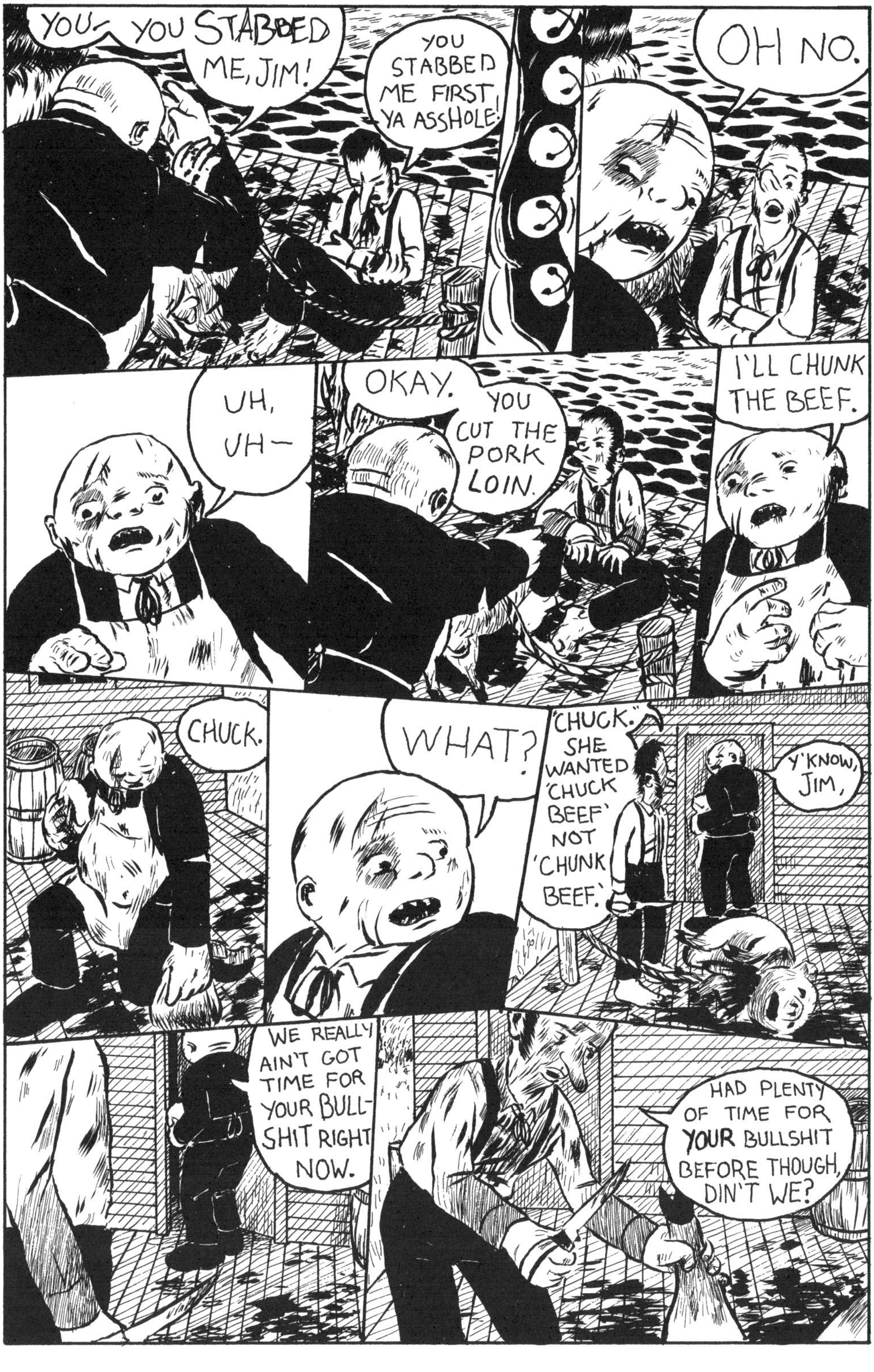

YOU- YOU STABBED ME, JIM!
YOU STABBED ME FIRST YA ASSHOLE!
OH NO.
UH, UH—
OKAY.
YOU CUT THE PORK LOIN.
I'LL CHUNK THE BEEF.
CHUCK.
WHAT?
"CHUCK." SHE WANTED 'CHUCK BEEF' NOT 'CHUNK BEEF.'
Y'KNOW, JIM,
WE REALLY AIN'T GOT TIME FOR YOUR BULL-SHIT RIGHT NOW.
HAD PLENTY OF TIME FOR YOUR BULLSHIT BEFORE THOUGH, DIN'T WE?

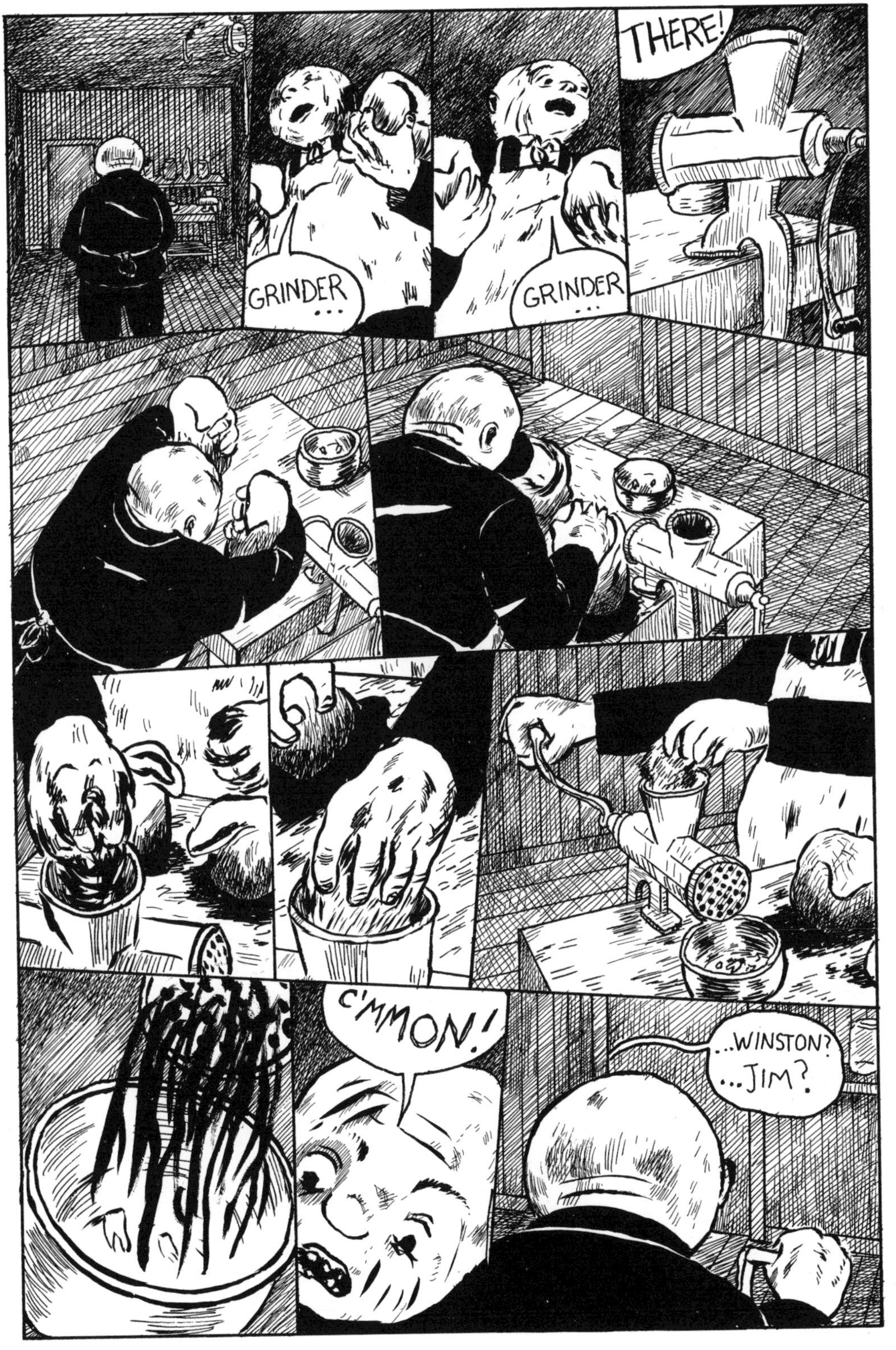
GRINDER
...
GRINDER
...
THERE!
C'MMON!
...WINSTON?
...JIM?

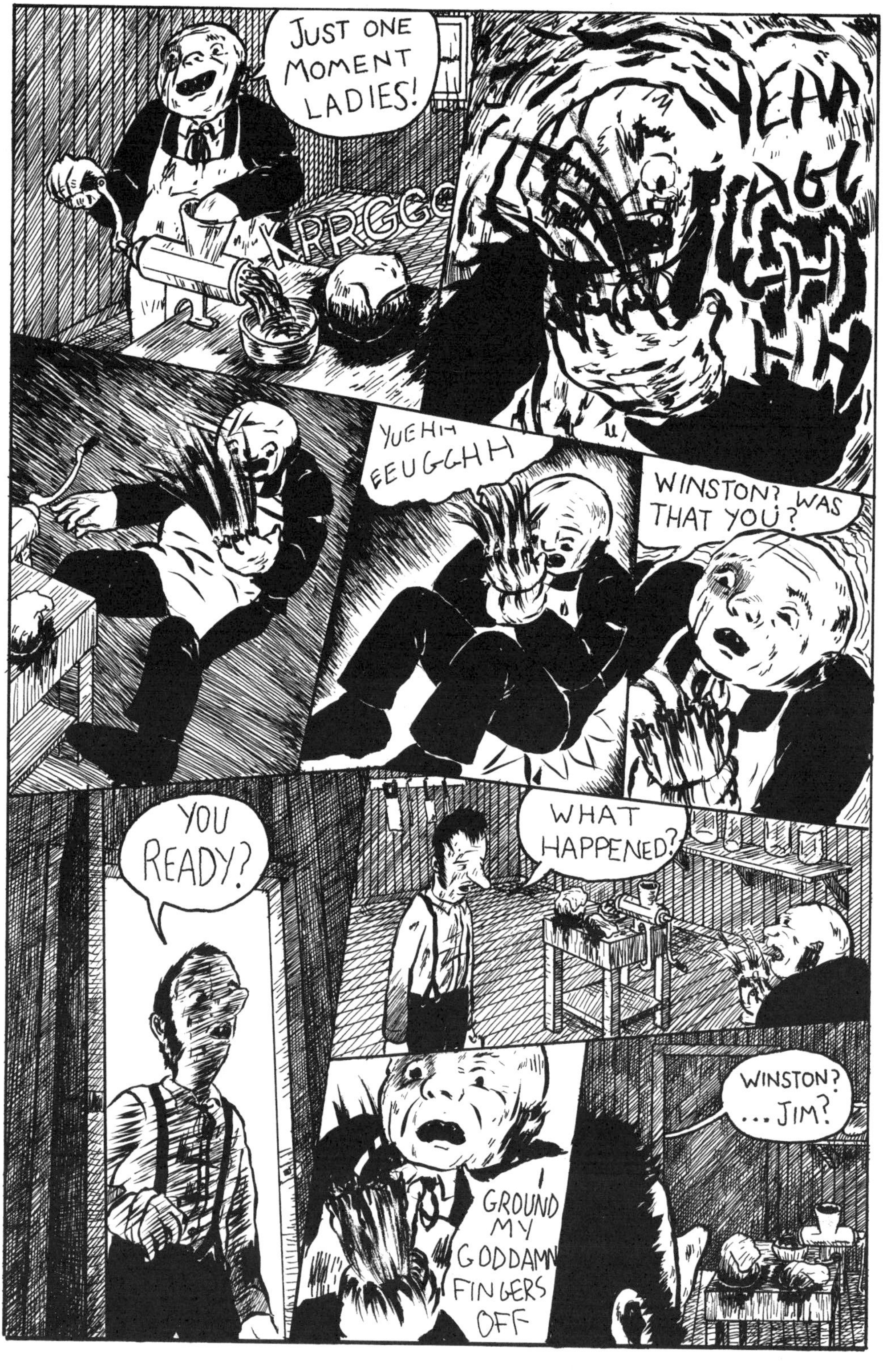
JUST ONE MOMENT LADIES!
KRRGGG
YUEHH EEUGGHH
WINSTON? WAS THAT YOU?
YOU READY?
WHAT HAPPENED?
I GROUND MY GODDAMN FINGERS OFF
WINSTON? ...JIM?

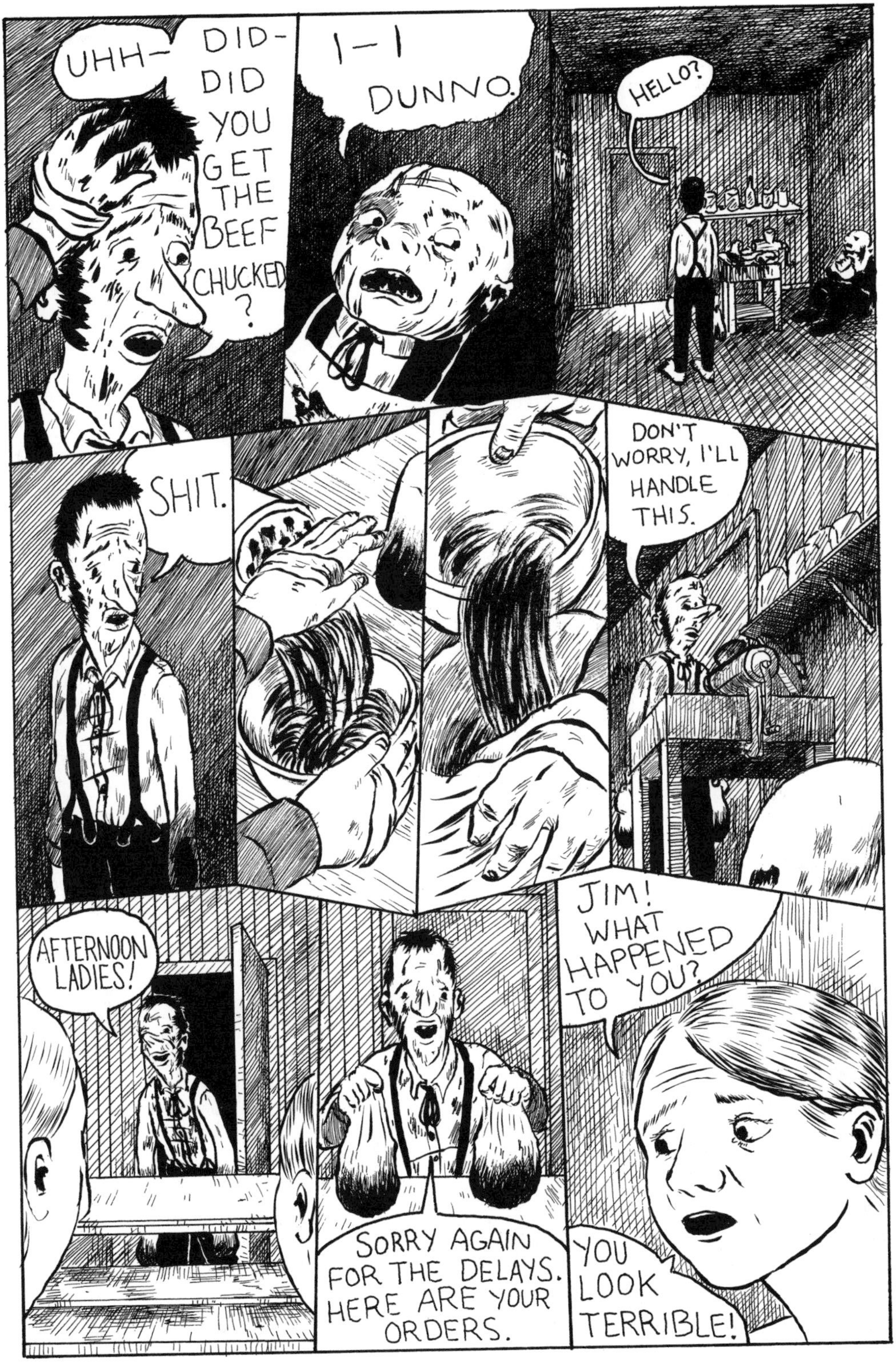
UHH-
DID- DID YOU GET THE BEEF CHUCKED?
I-I DUNNO.
HELLO?
SHIT.
DON'T WORRY, I'LL HANDLE THIS.
AFTERNOON LADIES!
SORRY AGAIN FOR THE DELAYS. HERE ARE YOUR ORDERS.
JIM! WHAT HAPPENED TO YOU?
YOU LOOK TERRIBLE!

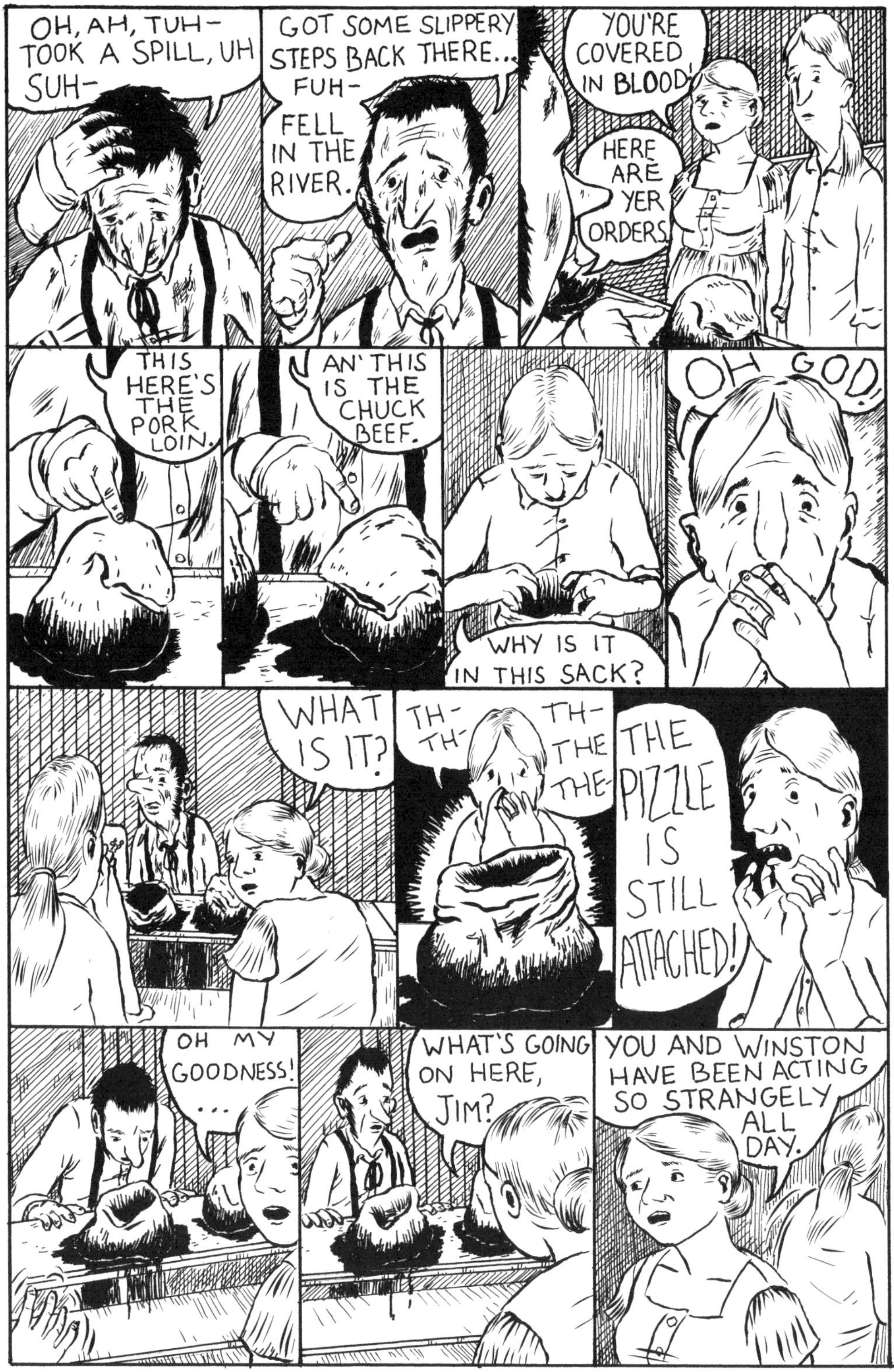
OH, AH, TUH- TOOK A SPILL, UH SUH-
GOT SOME SLIPPERY STEPS BACK THERE... FUH-
FELL IN THE RIVER.
YOU'RE COVERED IN BLOOD!
HERE ARE YER ORDERS.
THIS HERE'S THE PORK LOIN.
AN' THIS IS THE CHUCK BEEF.
WHY IS IT IN THIS SACK?
OH GOD!
WHAT IS IT?
TH- TH-
TH- THE THE-
THE PIZZLE IS STILL ATTACHED!
OH MY GOODNESS! ...
WHAT'S GOING ON HERE, JIM?
YOU AND WINSTON HAVE BEEN ACTING SO STRANGELY ALL DAY.

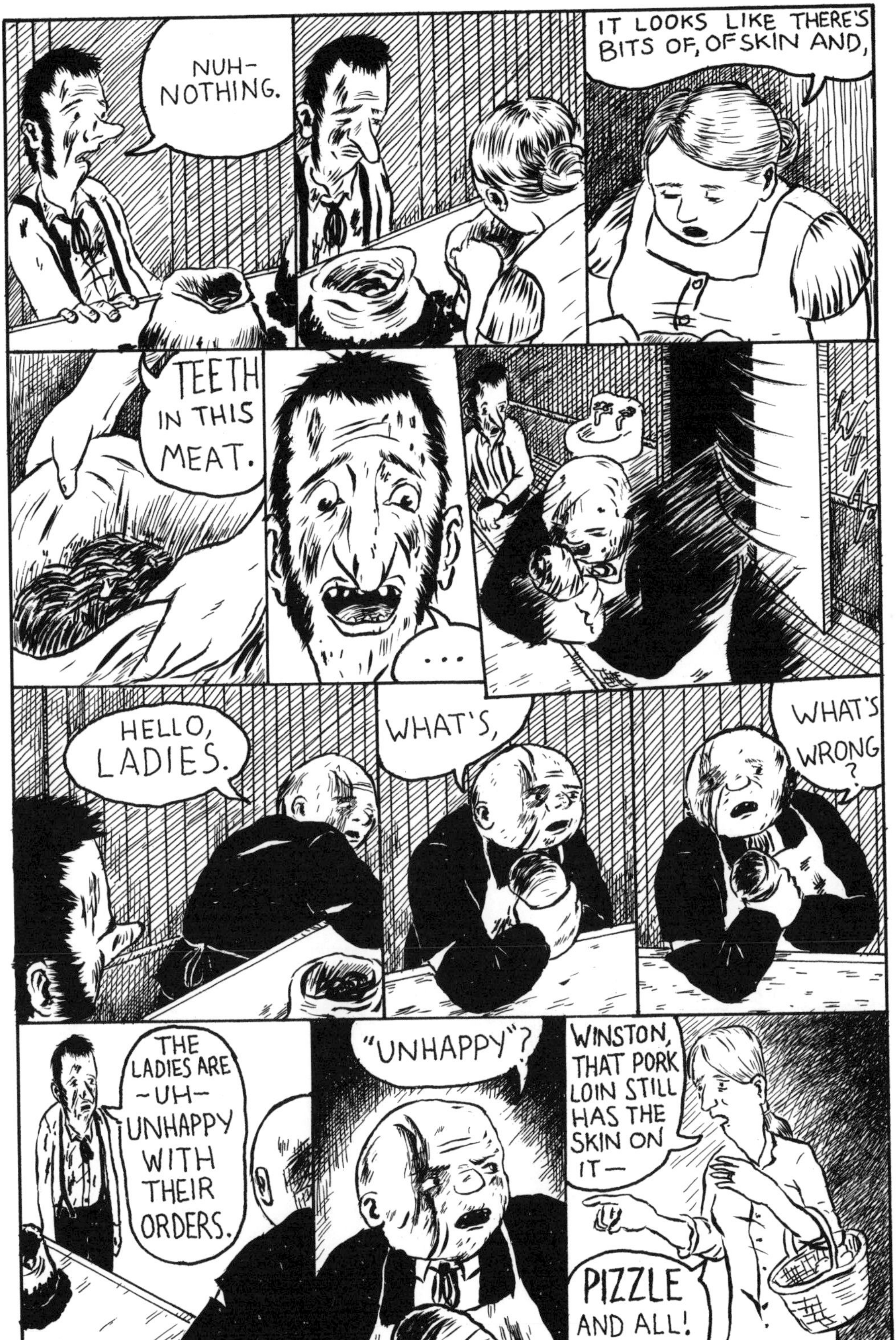
NUH-NOTHING.
IT LOOKS LIKE THERE'S BITS OF, OF SKIN AND,
TEETH IN THIS MEAT.
...
HELLO, LADIES.
WHAT'S,
WHAT'S WRONG?
THE LADIES ARE -UH- UNHAPPY WITH THEIR ORDERS.
"UNHAPPY"?
WINSTON, THAT PORK LOIN STILL HAS THE SKIN ON IT—
PIZZLE AND ALL!

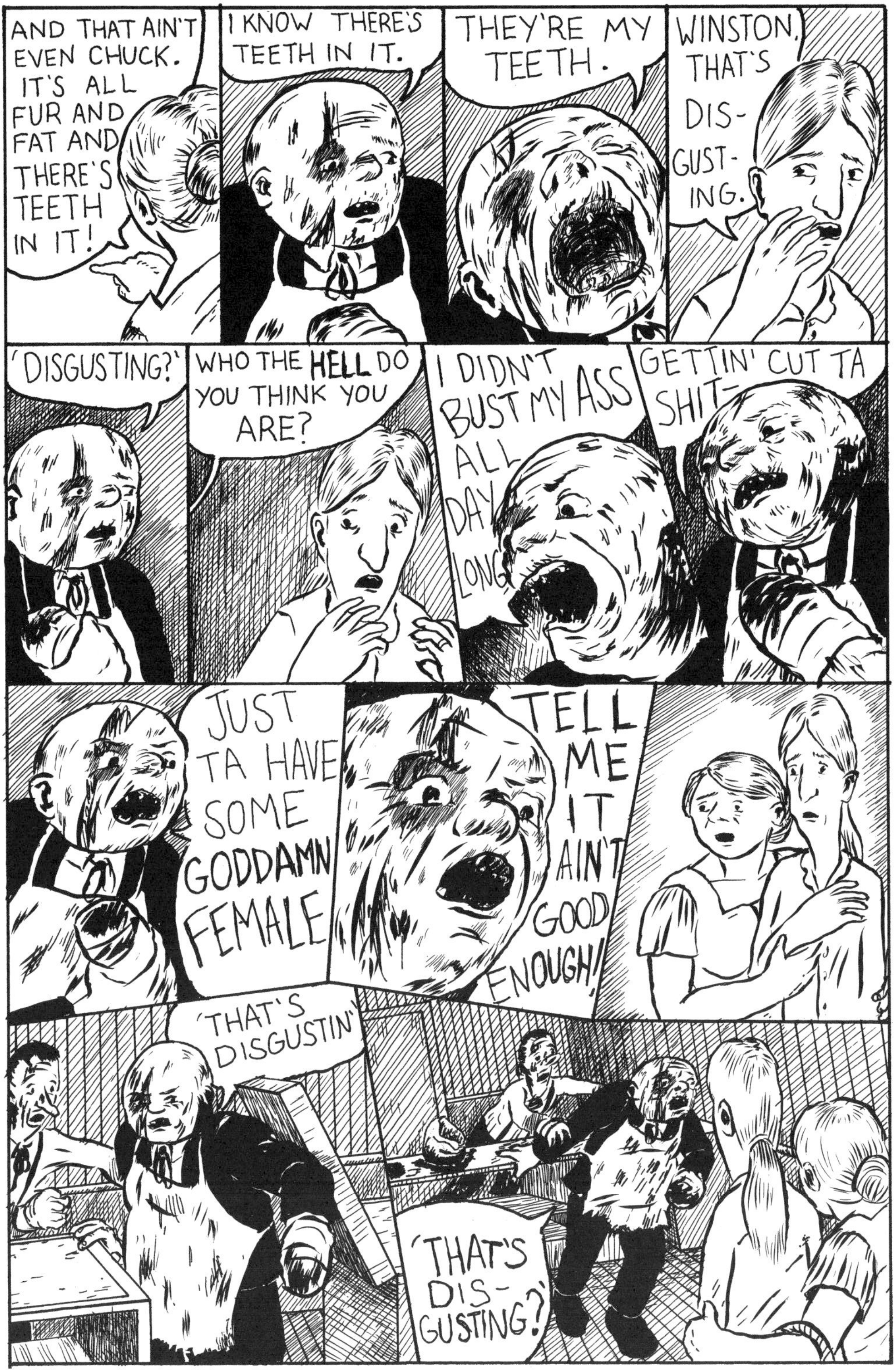
AND THAT AIN'T EVEN CHUCK. IT'S ALL FUR AND FAT AND THERE'S TEETH IN IT!
I KNOW THERE'S TEETH IN IT.
THEY'RE MY TEETH.
WINSTON, THAT'S DIS-GUST-ING.
'DISGUSTING?'
WHO THE HELL DO YOU THINK YOU ARE?
I DIDN'T BUST MY ASS ALL DAY LONG
GETTIN' CUT TA SHIT-
JUST TA HAVE SOME GODDAMN FEMALE
TELL ME IT AIN'T GOOD ENOUGH!
'THAT'S DISGUSTIN'
'THAT'S DIS-GUSTING?'

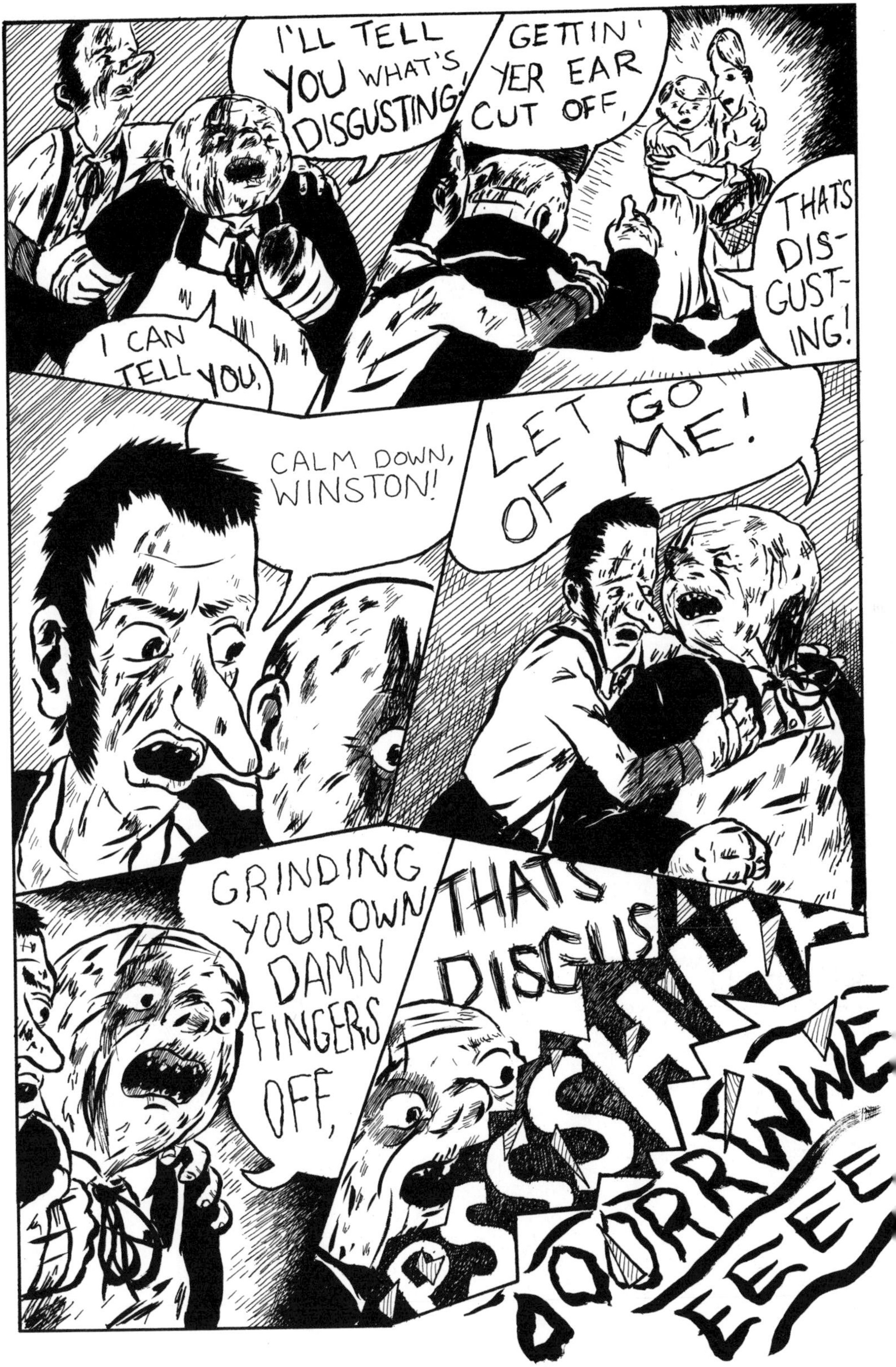
I'LL TELL YOU WHAT'S DISGUSTING!
I CAN TELL YOU,
GETTIN' YER EAR CUT OFF,
THAT'S DIS-GUST-ING!
CALM DOWN, WINSTON!
LET GO OF ME!
GRINDING YOUR OWN DAMN FINGERS OFF,
THATS DISGUS
SSHHHWWWEEEE

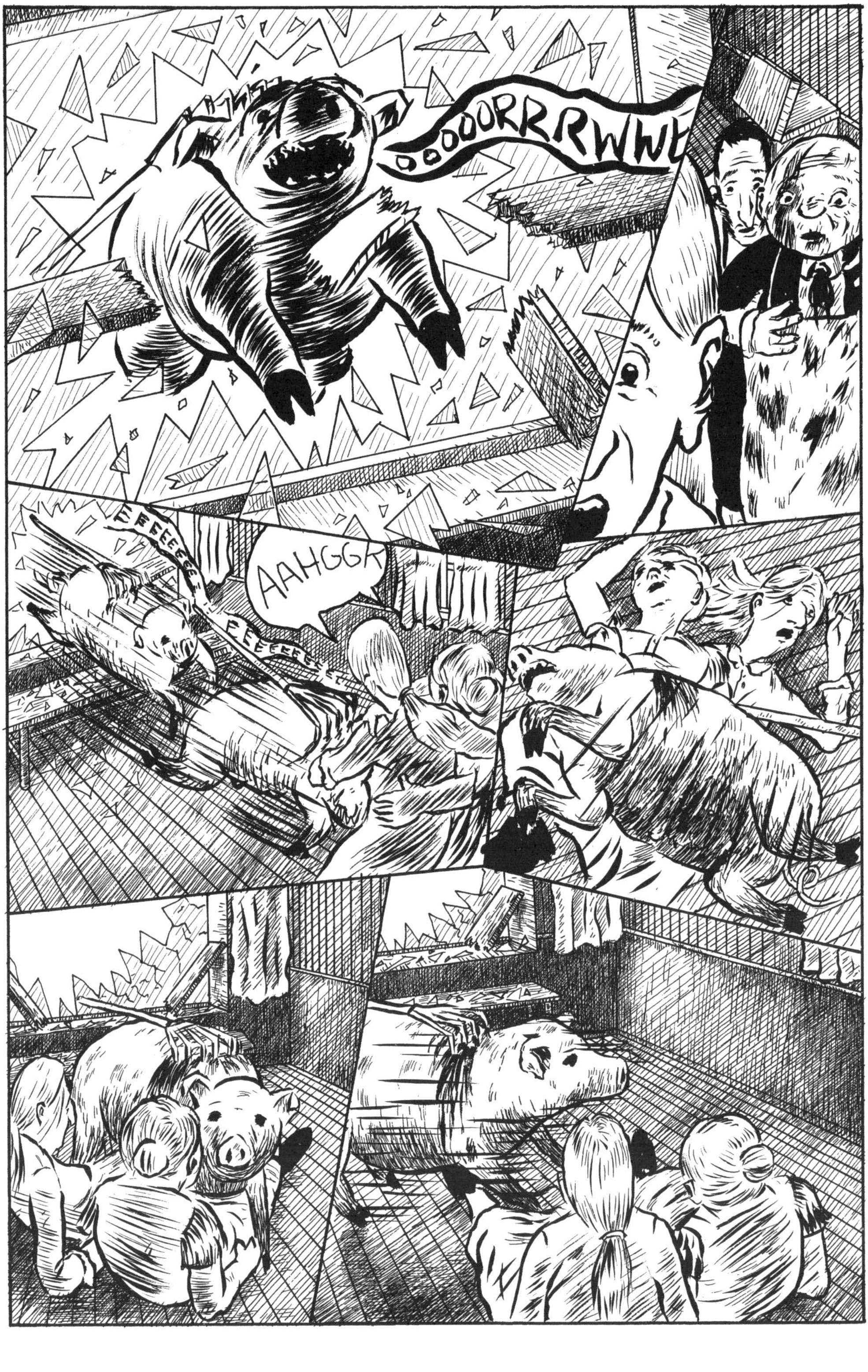
OOOOORRRRWWE
AAHGGR

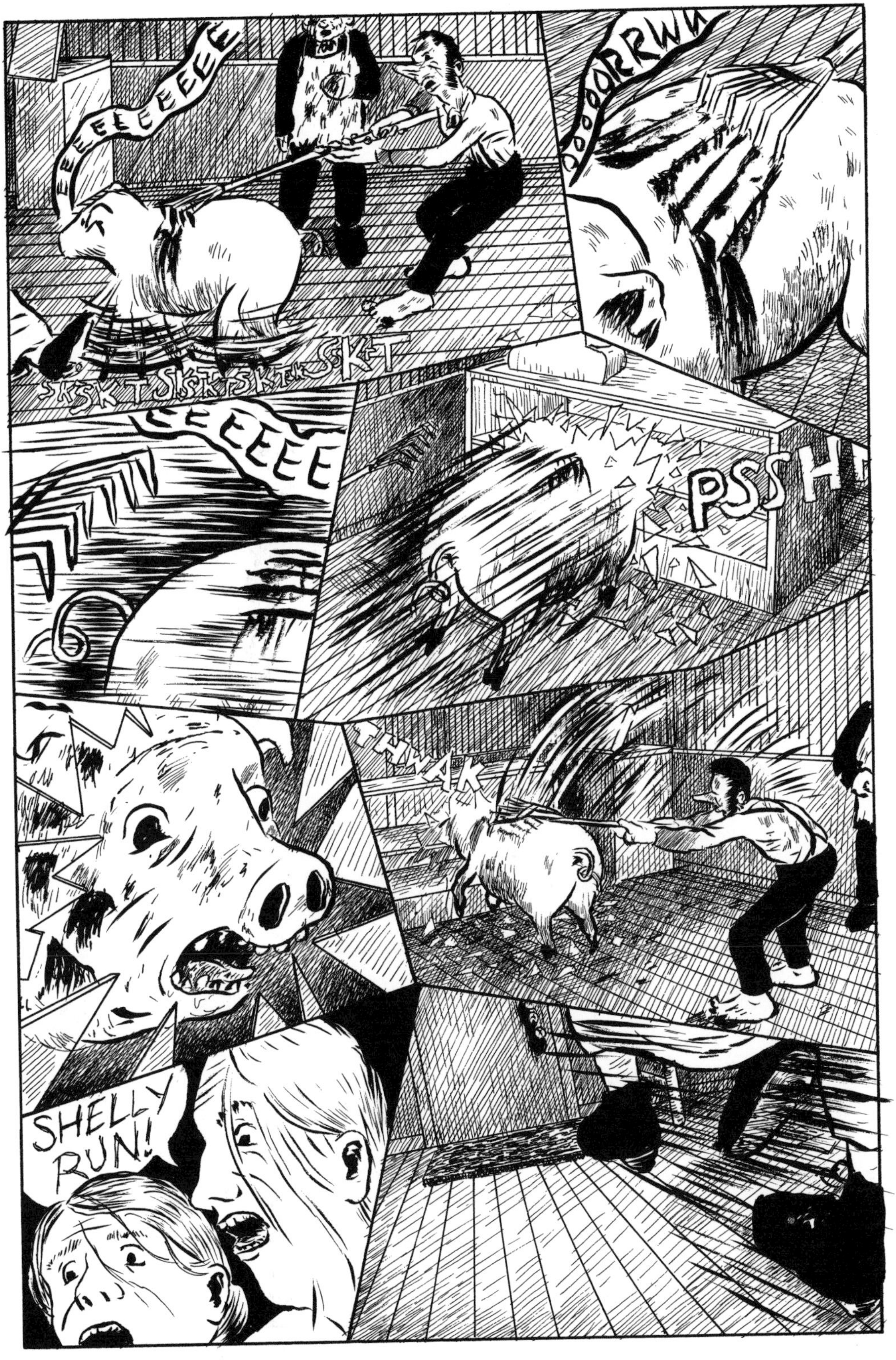
EEEEEEEEEEEE
OOOOOORRWN
EEEEE
PSSH
THWAK
SHELLY RUN!

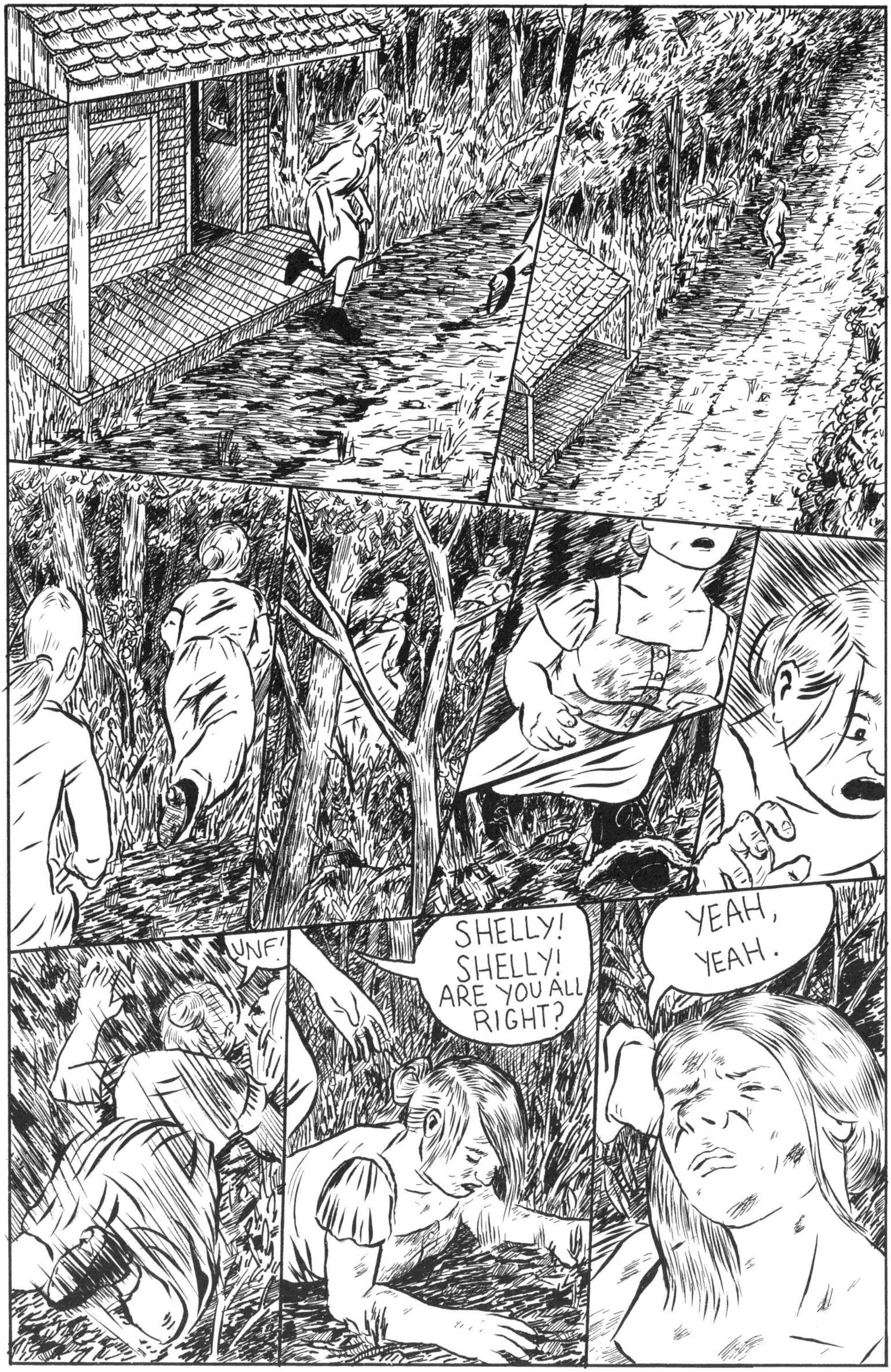
OPEN
UNF!
SHELLY! SHELLY! ARE YOU ALL RIGHT?
YEAH, YEAH.

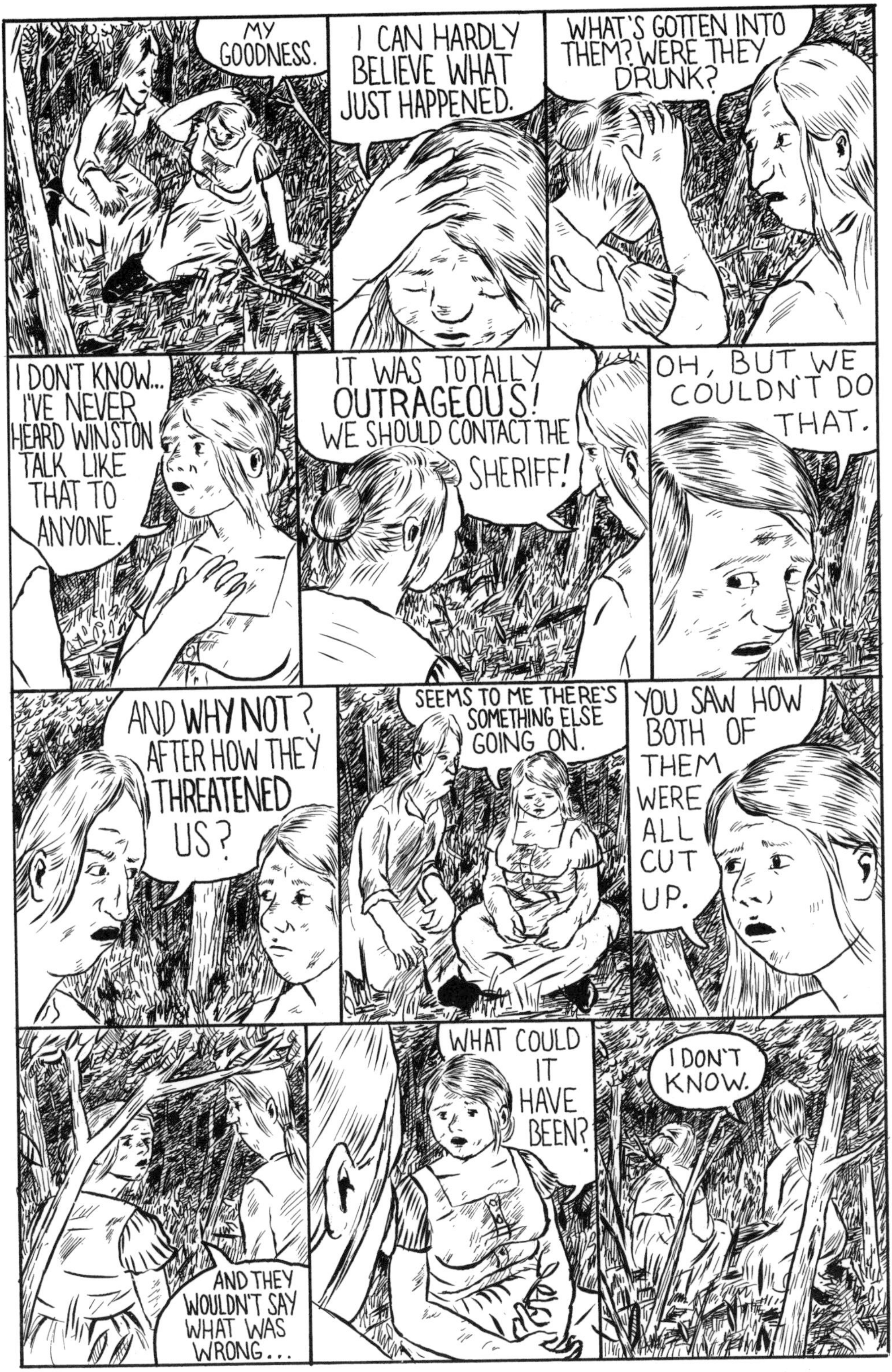
MY GOODNESS.
I CAN HARDLY BELIEVE WHAT JUST HAPPENED.
WHAT'S GOTTEN INTO THEM? WERE THEY DRUNK?
I DON'T KNOW... I'VE NEVER HEARD WINSTON TALK LIKE THAT TO ANYONE.
IT WAS TOTALLY OUTRAGEOUS! WE SHOULD CONTACT THE SHERIFF!
OH, BUT WE COULDN'T DO THAT.
AND WHY NOT? AFTER HOW THEY THREATENED US?
SEEMS TO ME THERE'S SOMETHING ELSE GOING ON.
YOU SAW HOW BOTH OF THEM WERE ALL CUT UP.
AND THEY WOULDN'T SAY WHAT WAS WRONG...
WHAT COULD IT HAVE BEEN?
I DON'T KNOW.

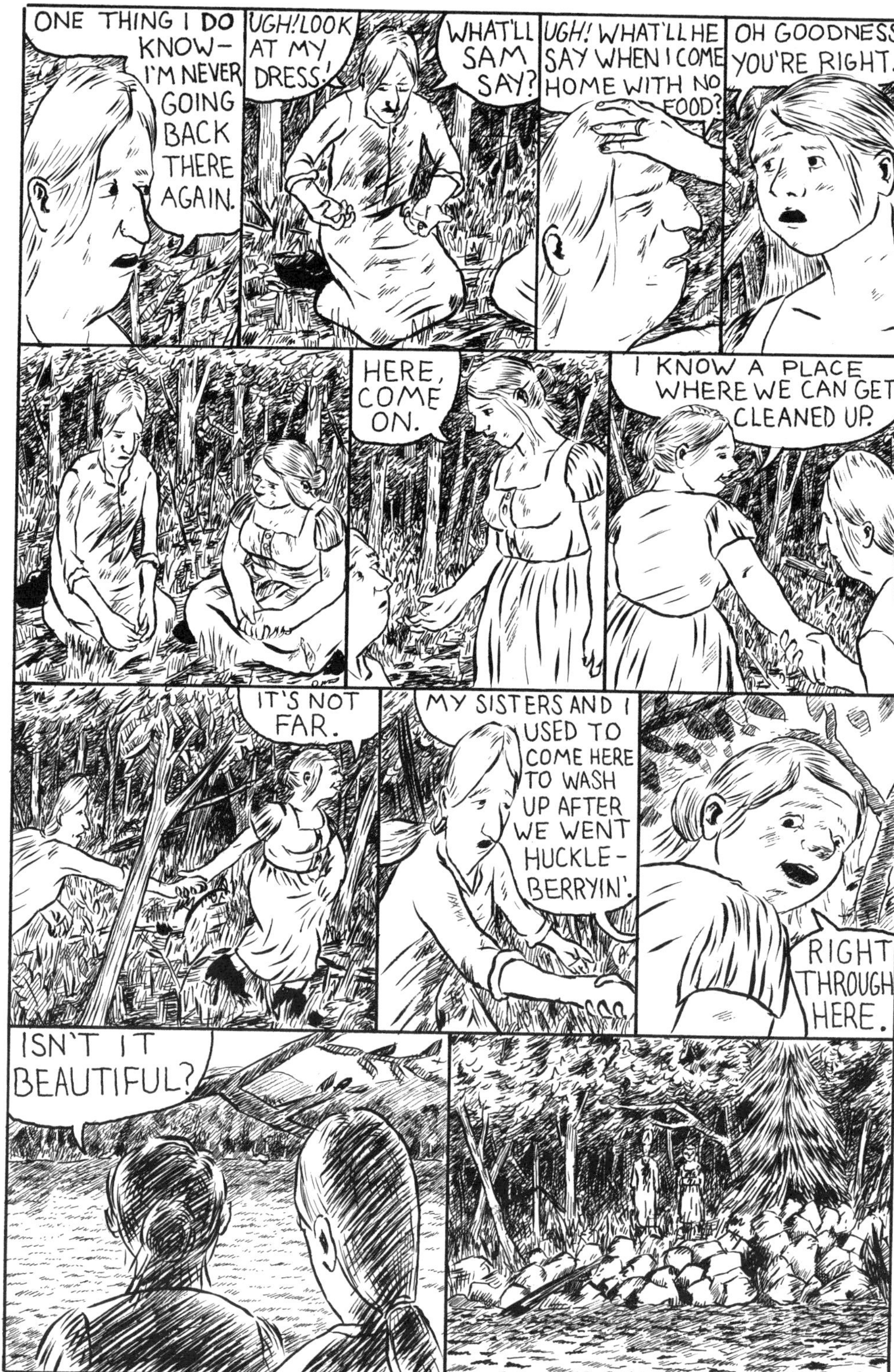
ONE THING I DO KNOW— I'M NEVER GOING BACK THERE AGAIN.
UGH! LOOK AT MY DRESS!
WHAT'LL SAM SAY?
UGH! WHAT'LL HE SAY WHEN I COME HOME WITH NO FOOD?
OH GOODNESS, YOU'RE RIGHT.
HERE, COME ON.
I KNOW A PLACE WHERE WE CAN GET CLEANED UP.
IT'S NOT FAR.
MY SISTERS AND I USED TO COME HERE TO WASH UP AFTER WE WENT HUCKLE-BERRYIN'.
RIGHT THROUGH HERE.
ISN'T IT BEAUTIFUL?

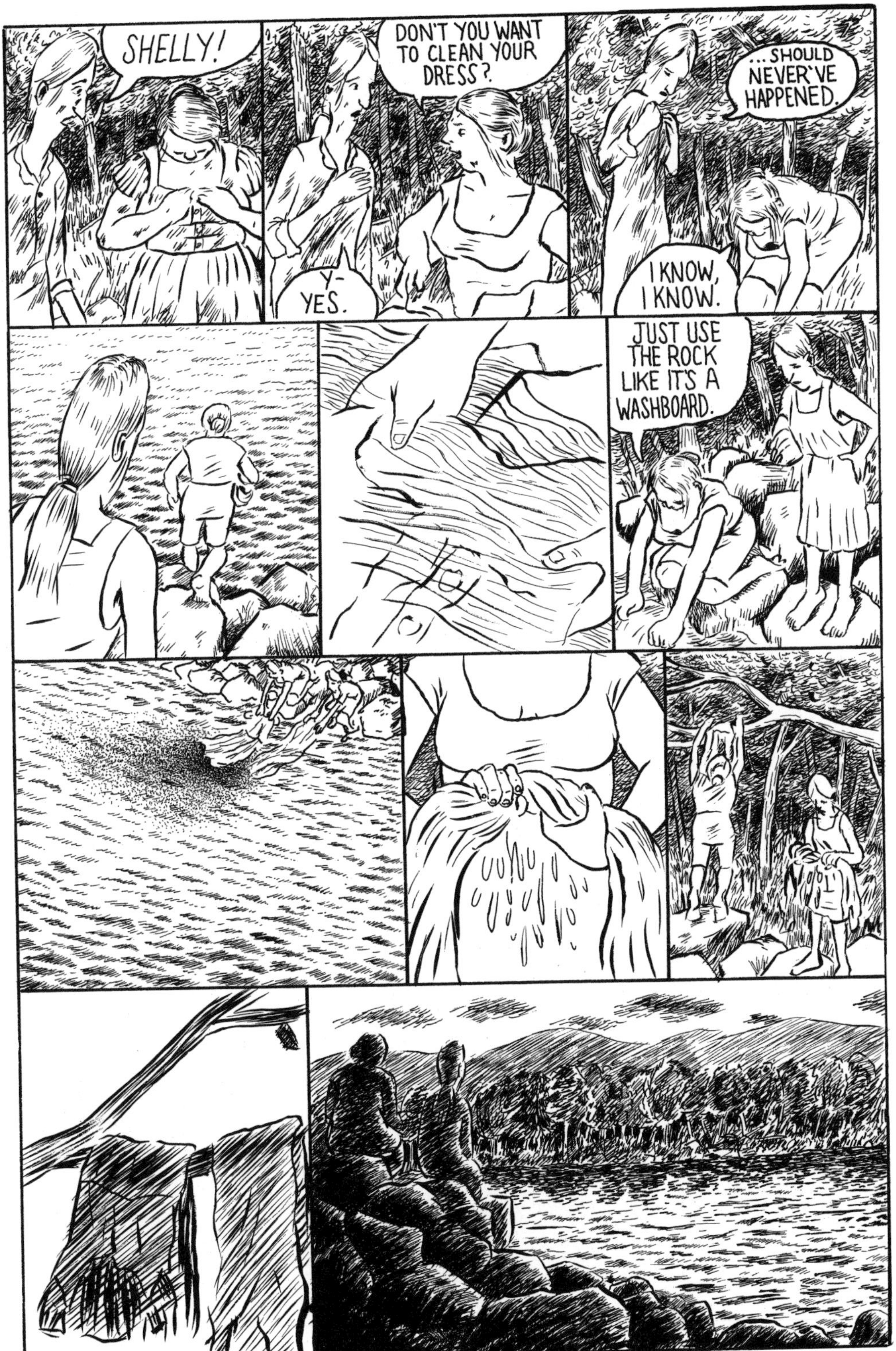
SHELLY!
DON'T YOU WANT TO CLEAN YOUR DRESS?
Y- YES.
...SHOULD NEVER'VE HAPPENED.
I KNOW, I KNOW.
JUST USE THE ROCK LIKE IT'S A WASHBOARD.

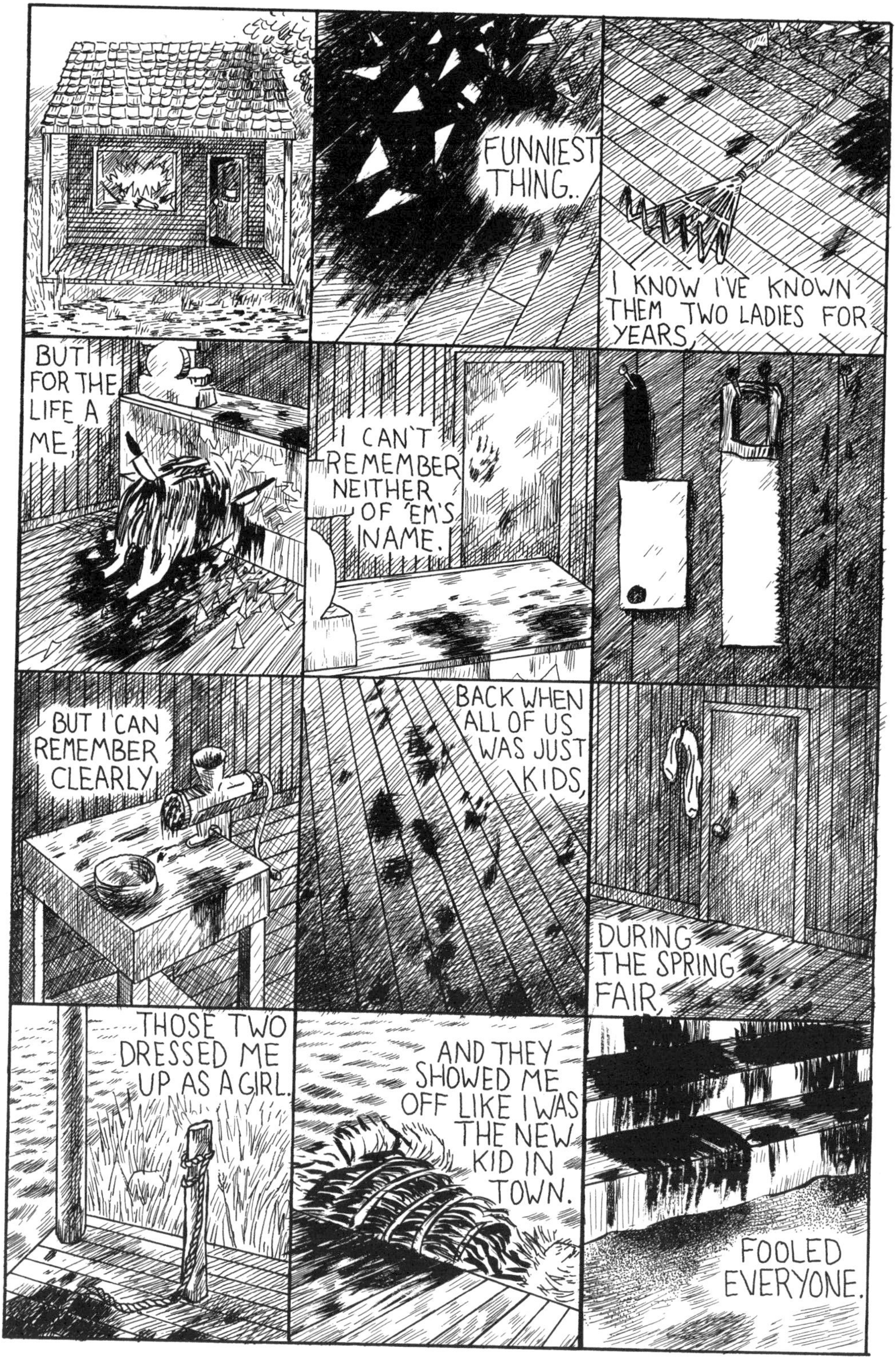
FUNNIEST THING..
I KNOW I'VE KNOWN THEM TWO LADIES FOR YEARS,
BUT FOR THE LIFE A ME,
I CAN'T REMEMBER NEITHER OF 'EM'S NAME.
BUT I CAN REMEMBER CLEARLY
BACK WHEN ALL OF US WAS JUST KIDS,
DURING THE SPRING FAIR,
THOSE TWO DRESSED ME UP AS A GIRL.
AND THEY SHOWED ME OFF LIKE I WAS THE NEW KID IN TOWN.
FOOLED EVERYONE.

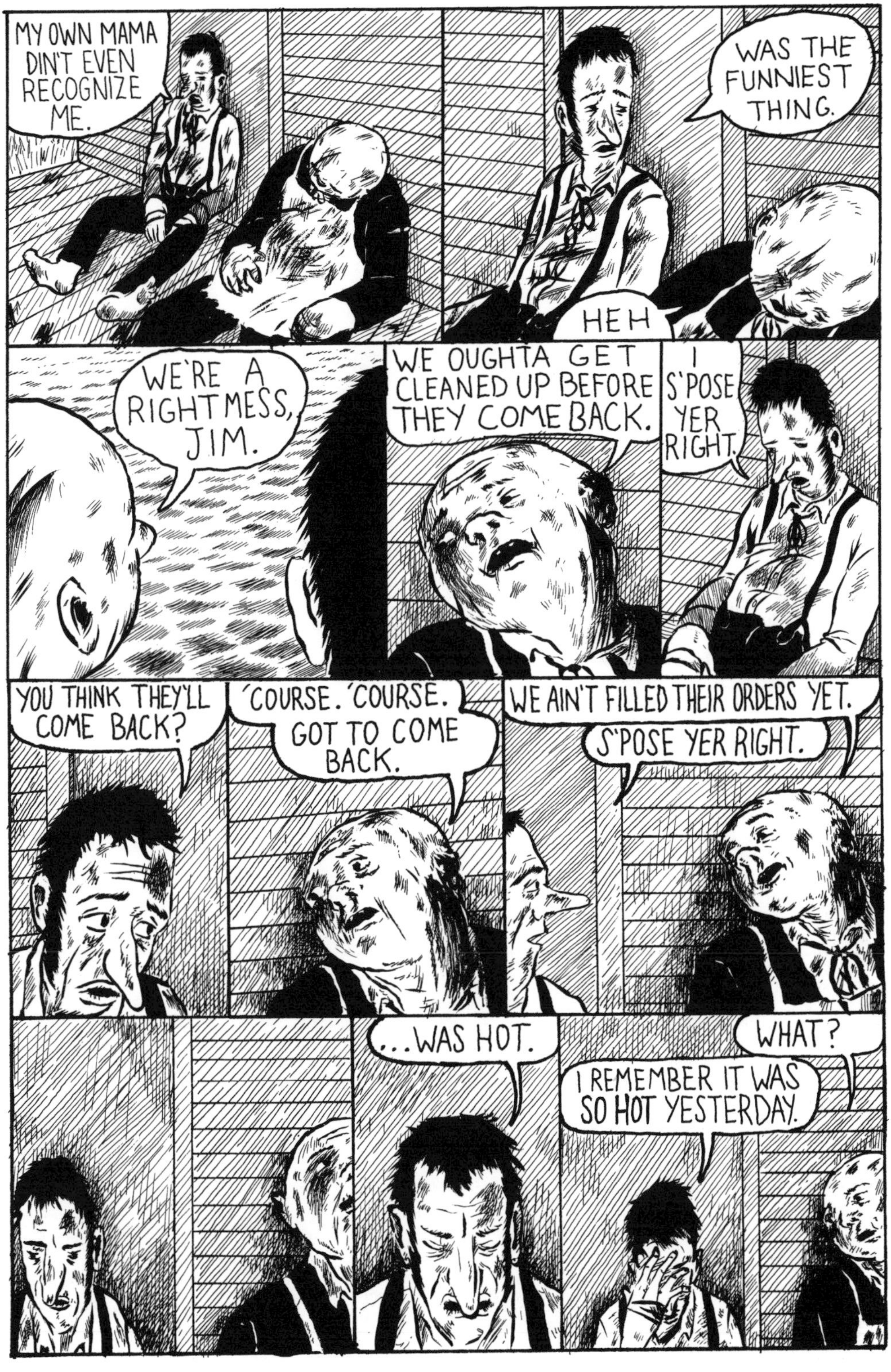
MY OWN MAMA DIN'T EVEN RECOGNIZE ME.
WAS THE FUNNIEST THING.
HEH
WE'RE A RIGHT MESS, JIM.
WE OUGHTA GET CLEANED UP BEFORE THEY COME BACK.
I S'POSE YER RIGHT.
YOU THINK THEY'LL COME BACK?
'COURSE. 'COURSE. GOT TO COME BACK.
WE AIN'T FILLED THEIR ORDERS YET.
S'POSE YER RIGHT.
...WAS HOT.
WHAT?
I REMEMBER IT WAS SO HOT YESTERDAY.

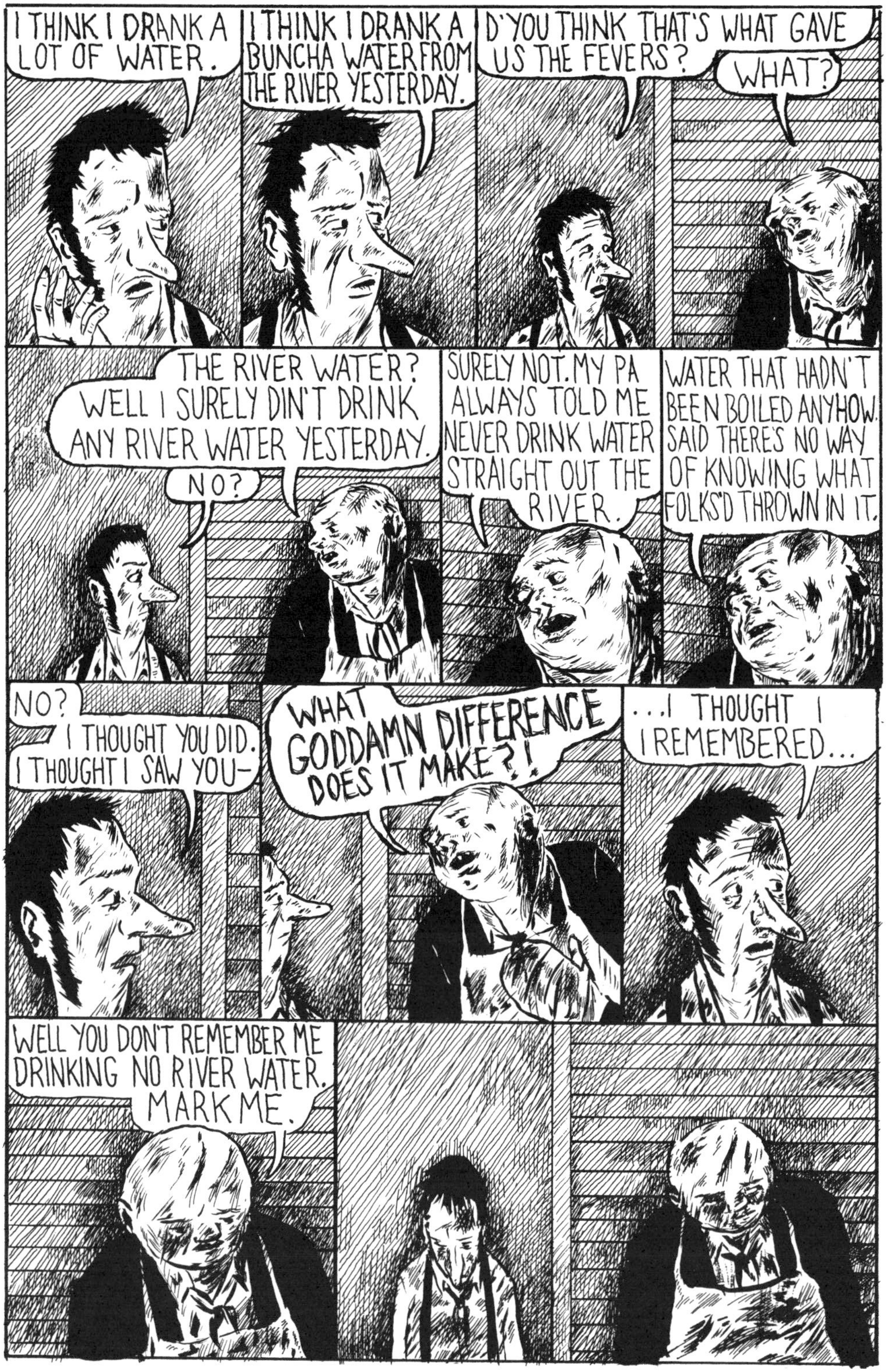
I THINK I DRANK A LOT OF WATER.
I THINK I DRANK A BUNCHA WATER FROM THE RIVER YESTERDAY.
D'YOU THINK THAT'S WHAT GAVE US THE FEVERS?
WHAT?
THE RIVER WATER? WELL I SURELY DIN'T DRINK ANY RIVER WATER YESTERDAY.
NO?
SURELY NOT. MY PA ALWAYS TOLD ME NEVER DRINK WATER STRAIGHT OUT THE RIVER.
WATER THAT HADN'T BEEN BOILED ANYHOW. SAID THERE'S NO WAY OF KNOWING WHAT FOLKS'D THROWN IN IT.
NO?
I THOUGHT YOU DID. I THOUGHT I SAW YOU-
WHAT GODDAMN DIFFERENCE DOES IT MAKE?!
...I THOUGHT I I REMEMBERED...
WELL YOU DON'T REMEMBER ME DRINKING NO RIVER WATER.
MARK ME.

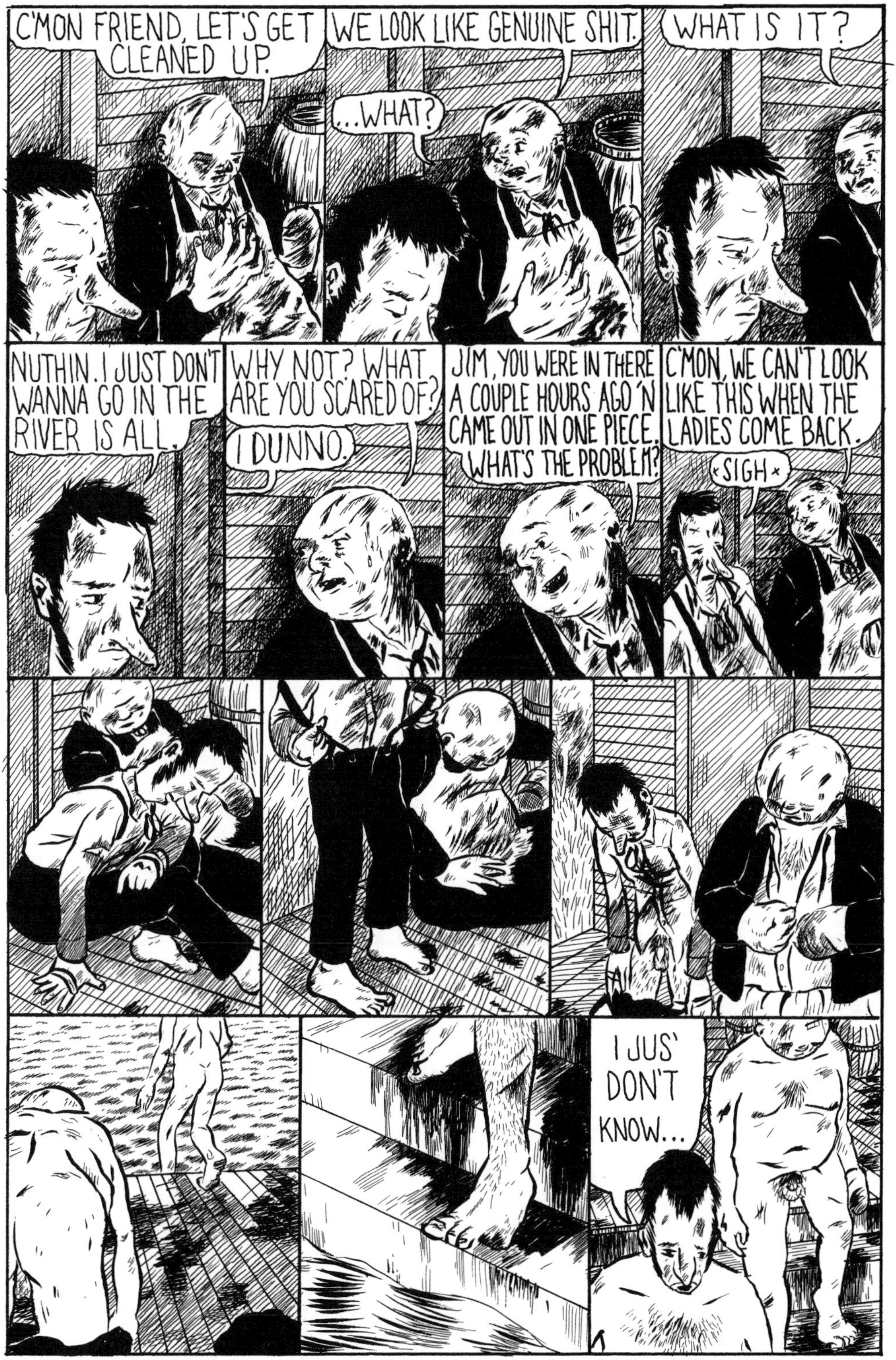
C'MON FRIEND, LET'S GET CLEANED UP.
WE LOOK LIKE GENUINE SHIT.
...WHAT?
WHAT IS IT?
NUTHIN. I JUST DON'T WANNA GO IN THE RIVER IS ALL.
WHY NOT? WHAT, ARE YOU SCARED OF?
I DUNNO.
JIM, YOU WERE IN THERE A COUPLE HOURS AGO 'N CAME OUT IN ONE PIECE. WHAT'S THE PROBLEM?
C'MON, WE CAN'T LOOK LIKE THIS WHEN THE LADIES COME BACK.
SIGH
I JUS' DON'T KNOW...

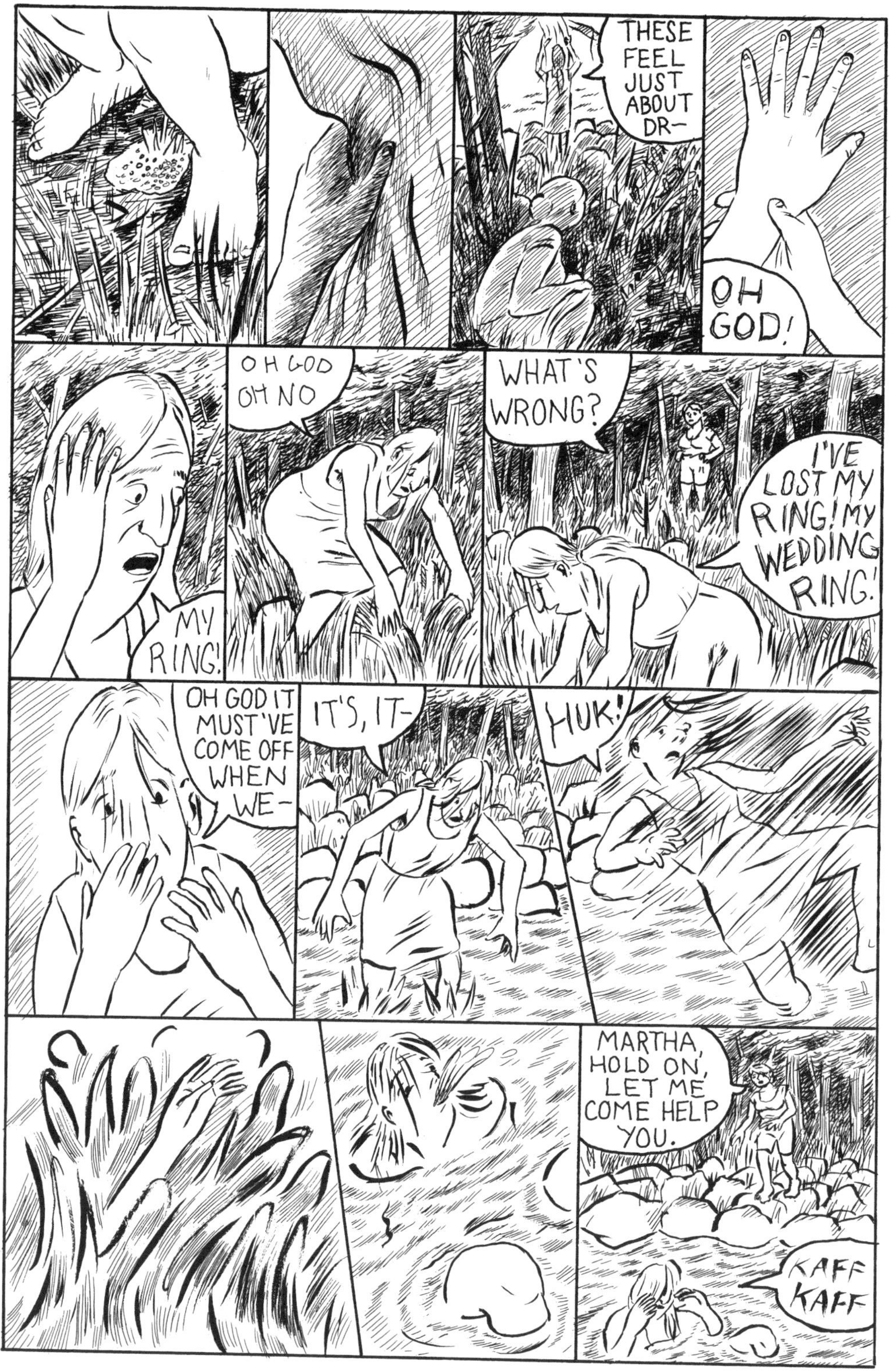
THESE FEEL JUST ABOUT DR-
OH GOD!
MY RING!
OH GOD OH NO
WHAT'S WRONG?
I'VE LOST MY RING! MY WEDDING RING!
OH GOD IT MUST'VE COME OFF WHEN WE-
IT'S, IT-
HUK!
MARTHA, HOLD ON, LET ME COME HELP YOU.
KAFF KAFF

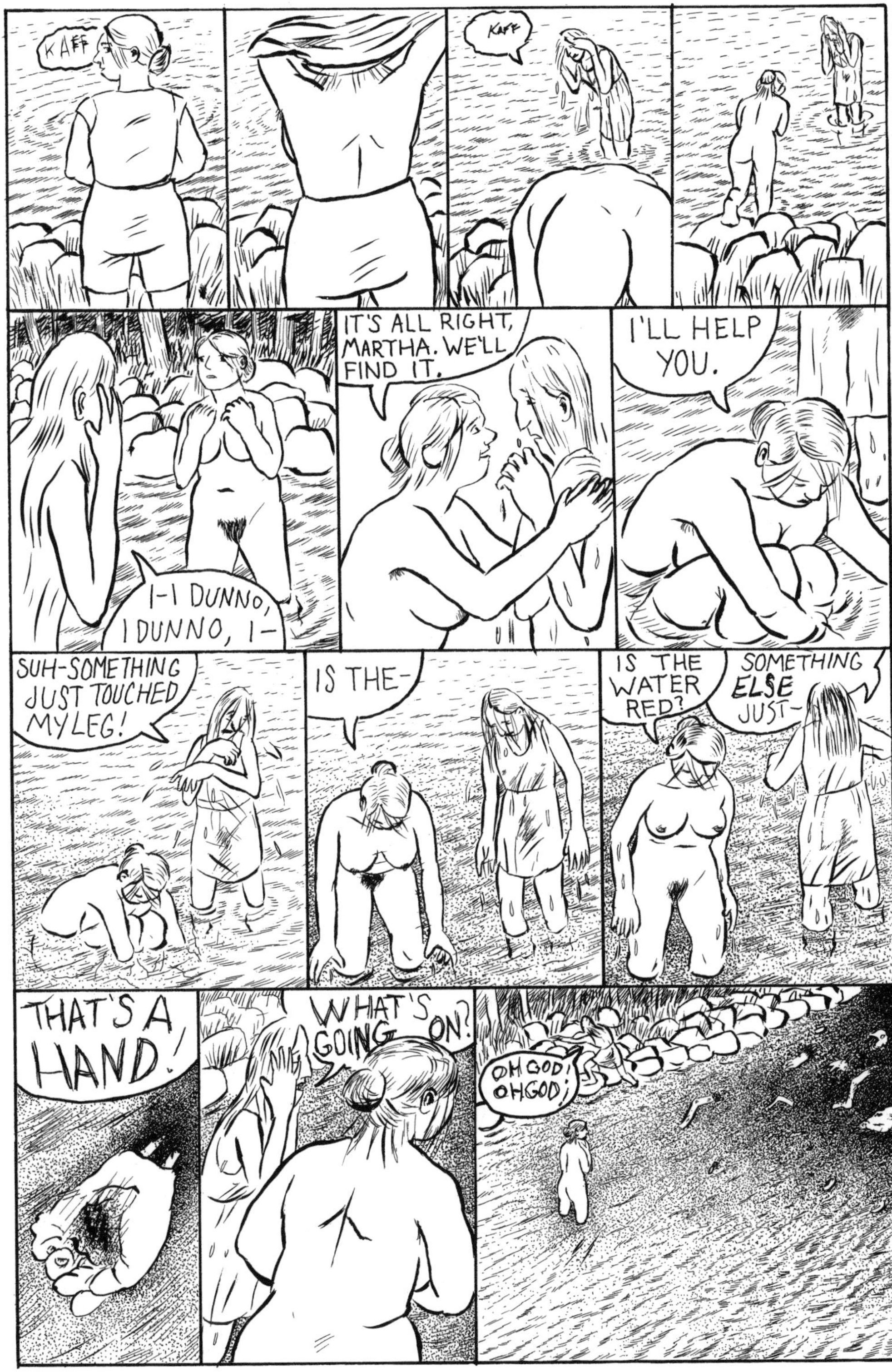
KAFF
KAFF
I-I DUNNO, I DUNNO, I-
IT'S ALL RIGHT, MARTHA. WE'LL FIND IT.
I'LL HELP YOU.
SUH-SOMETHING JUST TOUCHED MY LEG!
IS THE-
IS THE WATER RED?
SOMETHING ELSE JUST-
THAT'S A HAND!
WHAT'S GOING ON?
OH GOD! OH GOD!

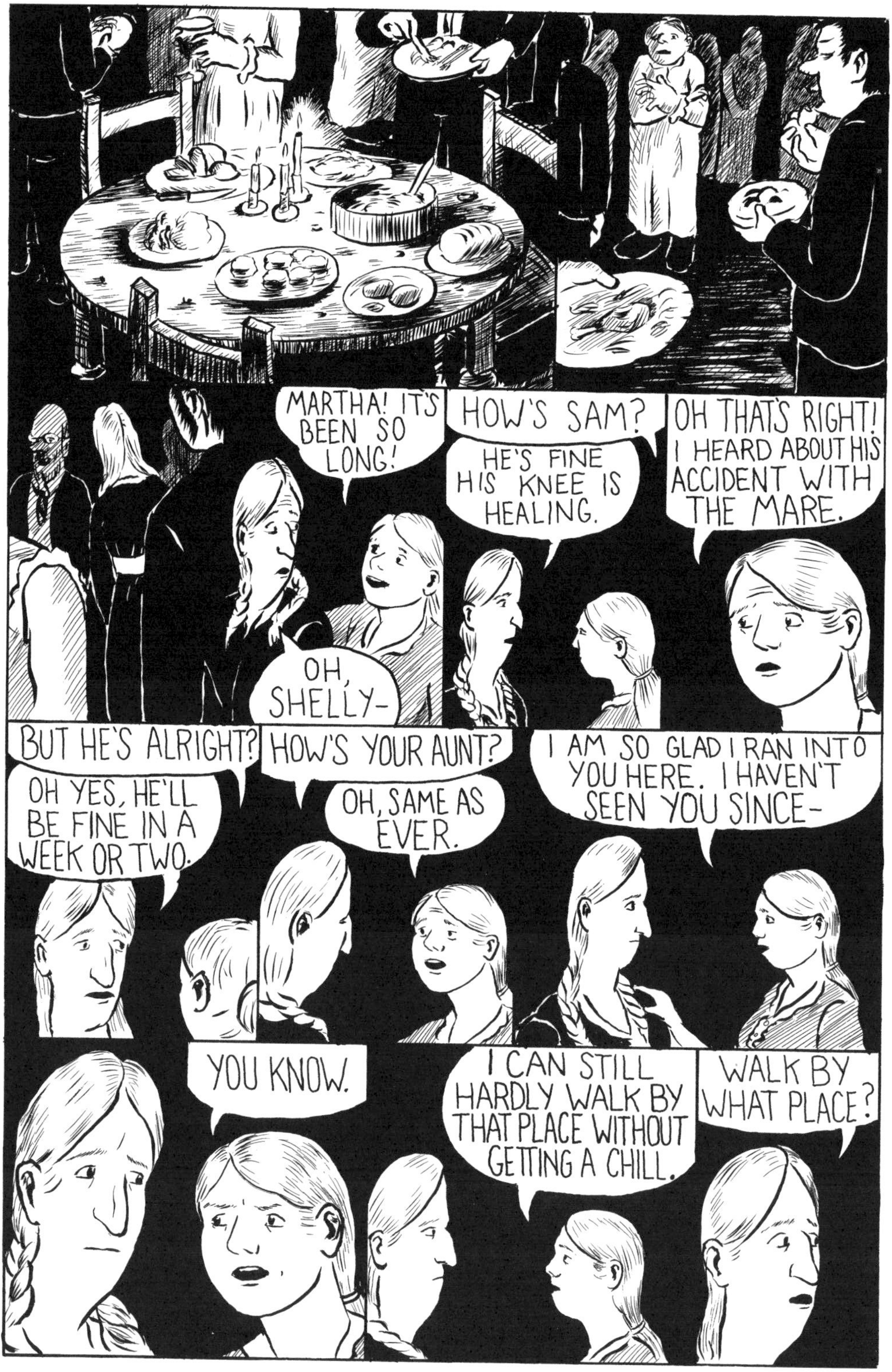
MARTHA! IT'S BEEN SO LONG!
OH, SHELLY-
HOW'S SAM?
HE'S FINE HIS KNEE IS HEALING.
OH THAT'S RIGHT! I HEARD ABOUT HIS ACCIDENT WITH THE MARE.
BUT HE'S ALRIGHT?
OH YES, HE'LL BE FINE IN A WEEK OR TWO.
HOW'S YOUR AUNT?
OH, SAME AS EVER.
I AM SO GLAD I RAN INTO YOU HERE. I HAVEN'T SEEN YOU SINCE-
YOU KNOW.
I CAN STILL HARDLY WALK BY THAT PLACE WITHOUT GETTING A CHILL.
WALK BY WHAT PLACE?

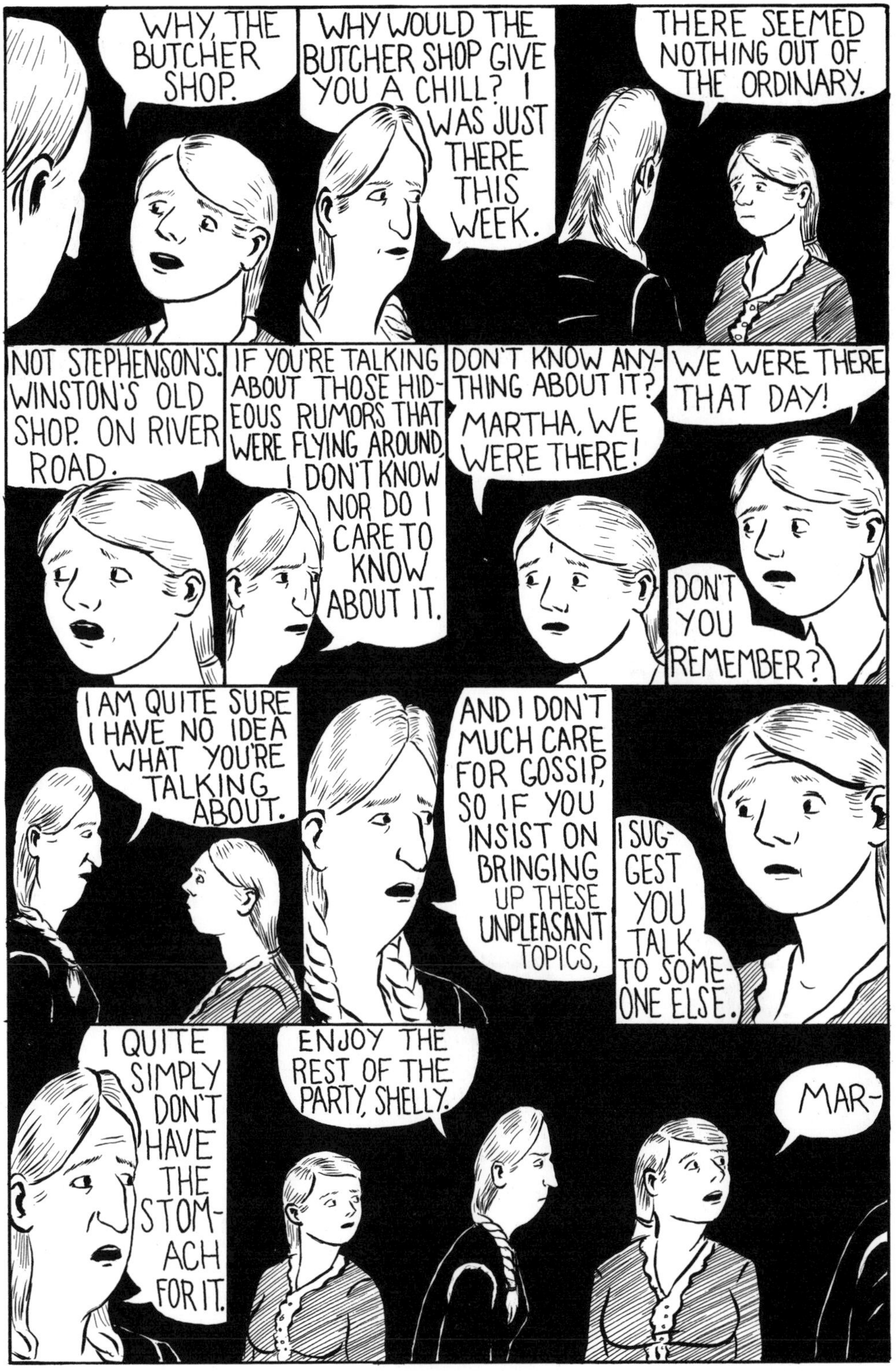
WHY, THE BUTCHER SHOP.
WHY WOULD THE BUTCHER SHOP GIVE YOU A CHILL? I WAS JUST THERE THIS WEEK.
THERE SEEMED NOTHING OUT OF THE ORDINARY.
NOT STEPHENSON'S. WINSTON'S OLD SHOP. ON RIVER ROAD.
IF YOU'RE TALKING ABOUT THOSE HIDEOUS RUMORS THAT WERE FLYING AROUND, I DON'T KNOW NOR DO I CARE TO KNOW ABOUT IT.
DON'T KNOW ANYTHING ABOUT IT?
MARTHA, WE WERE THERE!
WE WERE THERE THAT DAY!
DON'T YOU REMEMBER?
I AM QUITE SURE I HAVE NO IDEA WHAT YOU'RE TALKING ABOUT.
AND I DON'T MUCH CARE FOR GOSSIP, SO IF YOU INSIST ON BRINGING UP THESE UNPLEASANT TOPICS,
I SUGGEST YOU TALK TO SOMEONE ELSE.
I QUITE SIMPLY DON'T HAVE THE STOMACH FOR IT.
ENJOY THE REST OF THE PARTY, SHELLY.
MAR-

MAY 17, XXXX

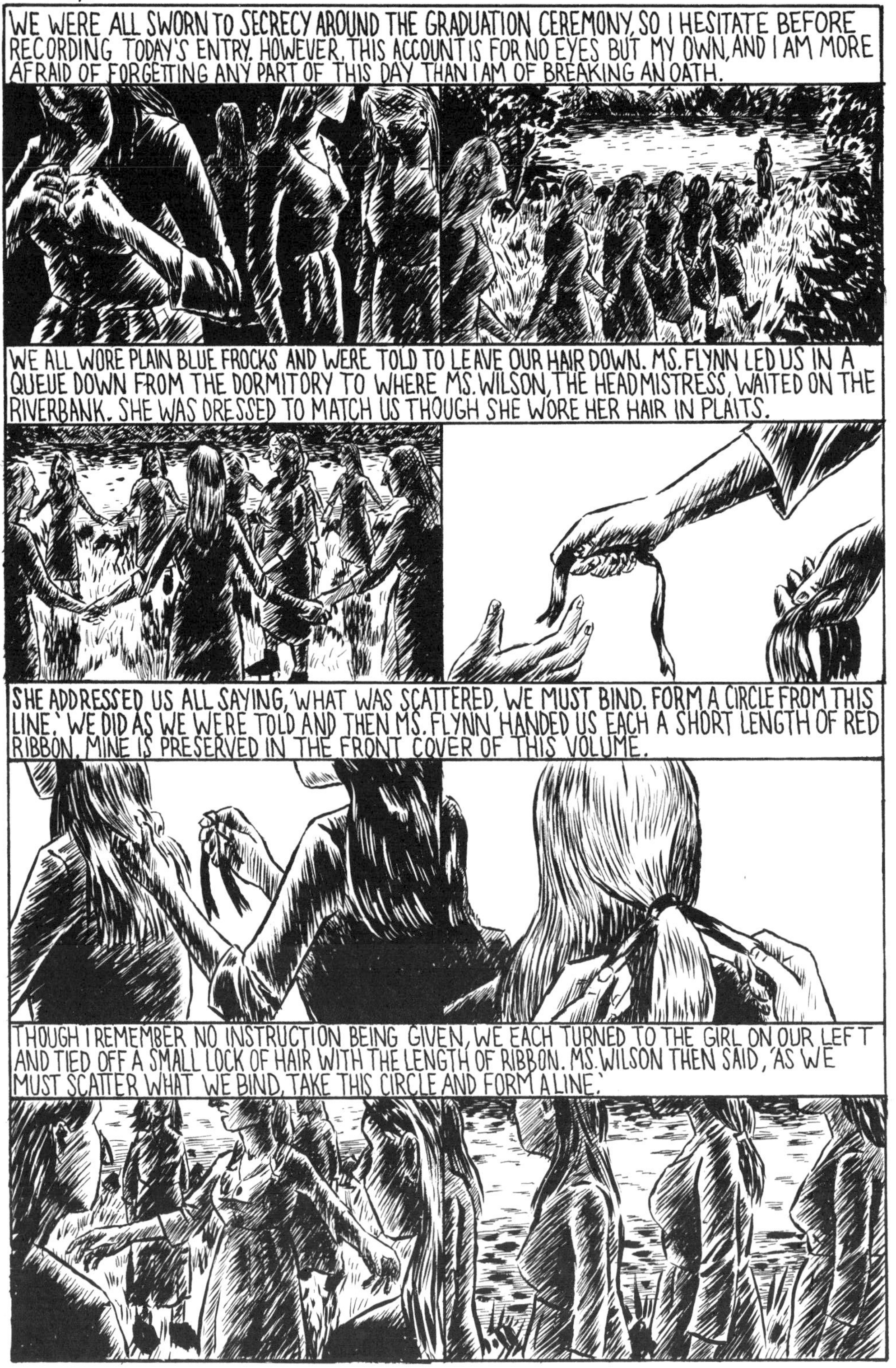
WE WERE ALL SWORN TO SECRECY AROUND THE GRADUATION CEREMONY, SO I HESITATE BEFORE RECORDING TODAY'S ENTRY. HOWEVER, THIS ACCOUNT IS FOR NO EYES BUT MY OWN, AND I AM MORE AFRAID OF FORGETTING ANY PART OF THIS DAY THAN I AM OF BREAKING AN OATH.
WE ALL WORE PLAIN BLUE FROCKS AND WERE TOLD TO LEAVE OUR HAIR DOWN. MS. FLYNN LED US IN A QUEUE DOWN FROM THE DORMITORY TO WHERE MS. WILSON, THE HEADMISTRESS, WAITED ON THE RIVERBANK. SHE WAS DRESSED TO MATCH US THOUGH SHE WORE HER HAIR IN PLAITS.
SHE ADDRESSED US ALL SAYING, 'WHAT WAS SCATTERED, WE MUST BIND. FORM A CIRCLE FROM THIS LINE.' WE DID AS WE WERE TOLD AND THEN MS. FLYNN HANDED US EACH A SHORT LENGTH OF RED RIBBON. MINE IS PRESERVED IN THE FRONT COVER OF THIS VOLUME.
THOUGH I REMEMBER NO INSTRUCTION BEING GIVEN, WE EACH TURNED TO THE GIRL ON OUR LEFT AND TIED OFF A SMALL LOCK OF HAIR WITH THE LENGTH OF RIBBON. MS. WILSON THEN SAID, 'AS WE MUST SCATTER WHAT WE BIND, TAKE THIS CIRCLE AND FORM A LINE.'

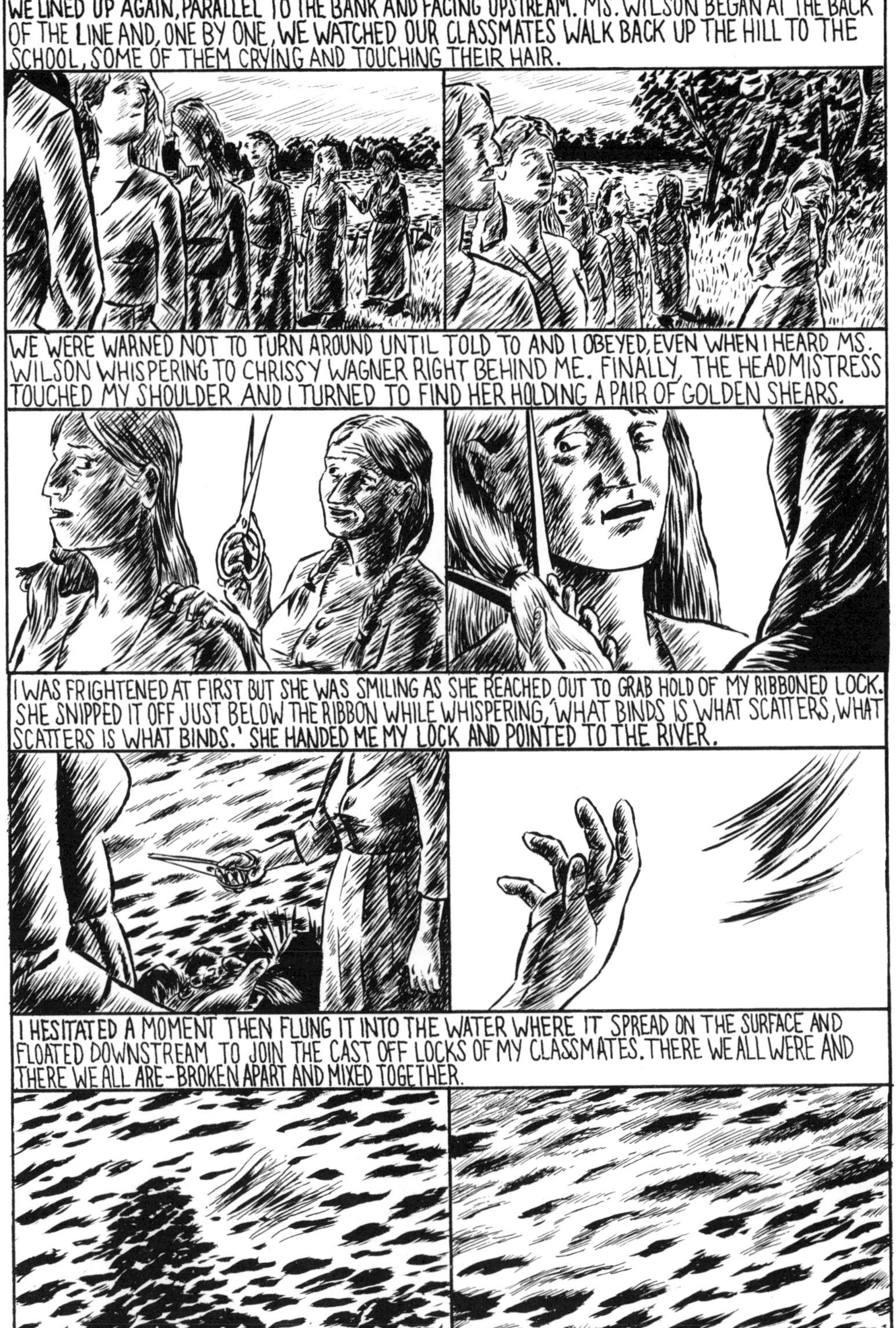
WE LINED UP AGAIN, PARALLEL TO THE BANK AND FACING UPSTREAM. MS. WILSON BEGAN AT THE BACK OF THE LINE AND, ONE BY ONE, WE WATCHED OUR CLASSMATES WALK BACK UP THE HILL TO THE SCHOOL, SOME OF THEM CRYING AND TOUCHING THEIR HAIR.
WE WERE WARNED NOT TO TURN AROUND UNTIL TOLD TO AND I OBEYED, EVEN WHEN I HEARD MS. WILSON WHISPERING TO CHRISSY WAGNER RIGHT BEHIND ME. FINALLY, THE HEADMISTRESS TOUCHED MY SHOULDER AND I TURNED TO FIND HER HOLDING A PAIR OF GOLDEN SHEARS.
I WAS FRIGHTENED AT FIRST BUT SHE WAS SMILING AS SHE REACHED OUT TO GRAB HOLD OF MY RIBBONED LOCK. SHE SNIPPED IT OFF JUST BELOW THE RIBBON WHILE WHISPERING, 'WHAT BINDS IS WHAT SCATTERS, WHAT SCATTERS IS WHAT BINDS.' SHE HANDED ME MY LOCK AND POINTED TO THE RIVER.
I HESITATED A MOMENT THEN FLUNG IT INTO THE WATER WHERE IT SPREAD ON THE SURFACE AND FLOATED DOWNSTREAM TO JOIN THE CAST OFF LOCKS OF MY CLASSMATES. THERE WE ALL WERE AND THERE WE ALL ARE - BROKEN APART AND MIXED TOGETHER.

CONOR STECHSCHULTE GREW UP IN RURAL PENNSYLVANIA. HE WAS EDUCATED AT THE INTERLOCHEN ARTS ACADEMY AND THE MARYLAND INSTITUTE COLLEGE OF ART. HE NOW LIVES WITH HIS GIRLFRIEND IN BALTIMORE WHERE, WHEN NOT DRAWING COMICS, HE PAINTS SMALL WATERCOLORS, HELPS TO RUN THE OPEN SPACE GALLERY, AND CUTS CHEESE FOR MONEY.

CONOR WOULD LIKE TO THANK MÁIRE, HIS BROTHER BEN, HIS PARENTS, DAY, FREIBERT, MILBURN, O'CONNELL, OPEN SPACE, ADAMS, BURKHOLDER, CLOUGH, DAVIDSON, FAKE, HARKHAM, MORRIS, NICHOLSON, RALPH, JTM AND REYNOLDS AND EVERYONE AT FANTAGRAPHICS WHO LENT TIME AND ENERGY TO THIS BOOK.

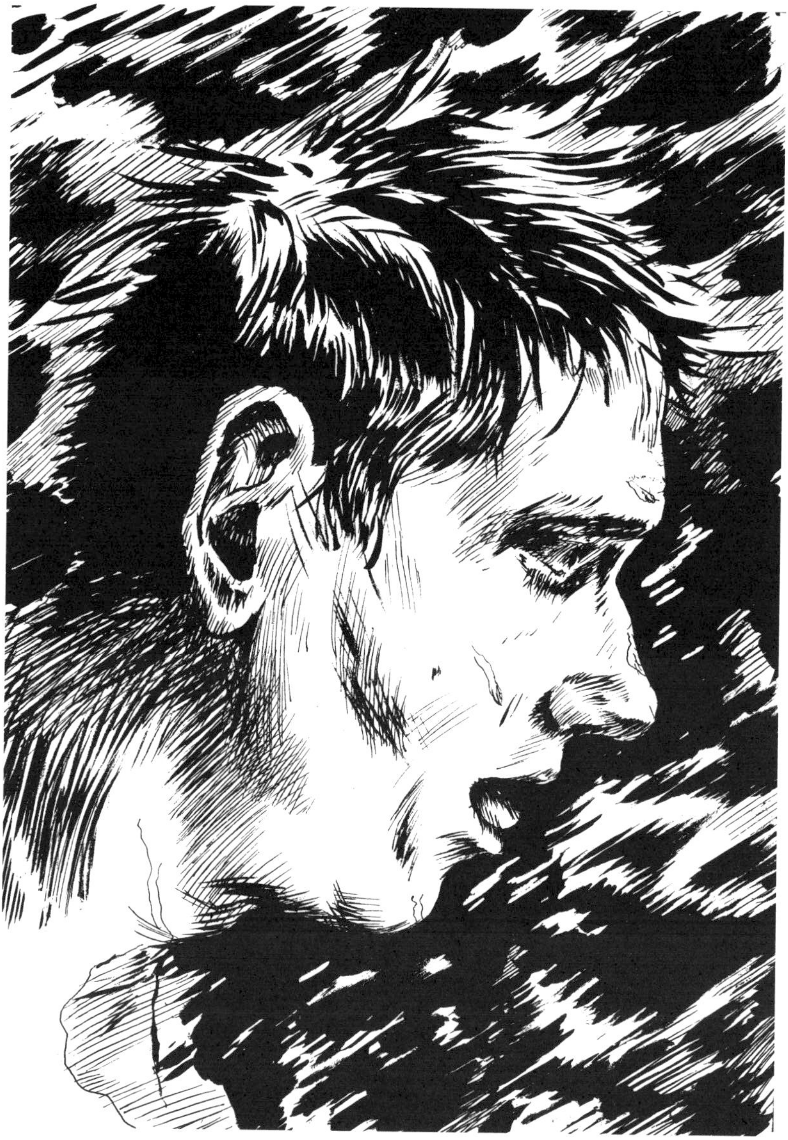